MUSTARD SEED FAITH

MUSTARD SEED FAITH

A Journey through Infertility, Miscarriages, Adoption, and Faith

Bethanee R. Syversen

ELM HILL

A Division of
HarperCollins Christian Publishing

www.elmhillbooks.com

Mustard Seed Faith
A Journey through Infertility, Miscarriages, Adoption, and Faith

Published in Nashville, Tennessee, by Elm Hill, an imprint of Thomas Nelson. Elm Hill and Thomas Nelson are registered trademarks of HarperCollins Christian Publishing, Inc.

Elm Hill titles may be purchased in bulk for educational, business, fund-raising, or sales promotional use. For information, please e-mail SpecialMarkets@ThomasNelson.com.

Scripture quotations marked AMP are from the Amplified® Bible. Copyright © 1954, 1958, 1962, 1964, 1965, 1987 by The Lockman Foundation. Used by permission. (www.Lockman.org)

Scripture quotations marked ESV are from the ESV® Bible (The Holy Bible, English Standard Version®). Copyright © 2001 by Crossway, a publishing ministry of Good News Publishers. Used by permission. All rights reserved.

Scripture quotations marked NCV are from the New Century Version®. © 2005 by Thomas Nelson. Used by permission. All rights reserved.

Scripture quotations marked NIV are from the Holy Bible, New International Version®, NIV®. Copyright © 1973, 1978, 1984, 2011 by Biblica, Inc.® Used by permission of Zondervan. All rights reserved worldwide. www.Zondervan.com. The "NIV" and "New International Version" are trademarks registered in the United States Patent and Trademark Office by Biblica, Inc.®

Scripture quotations marked NIRV are from the Holy Bible, New International Reader's Version®, NIRV®. Copyright ©1995, 1996, 1998, 2014 by Biblica, Inc.® Used by permission of Zondervan. All rights reserved worldwide. www.Zondervan.com. The "NIRV" and "New International Reader's Version" are trademarks registered in the United States Patent and Trademark Office by Biblica, Inc.®

Scripture quotations marked NLT are from the Holy Bible, New Living Translation. © 1996, 2004, 2007, 2013, 2015 by Tyndale House Foundation. Used by permission of Tyndale House Publishers, Inc., Carol Stream, Illinois 60188. All rights reserved.

Library of Congress Cataloging-in-Publication Data

Library of Congress Control Number: 2019934240

ISBN 978-1-400325337 (Paperback)
ISBN 978-1-400325344 (Hardbound)
ISBN 978-1-400325351 (eBook)

CONTENTS

DEDICATION

This book is dedicated to God, my Lord and Savior. Thank You for faithfully walking alongside me and for carrying me through the times I felt I couldn't walk myself. Your unwavering love and pursuit of me bring me to my knees in reverence, prayer, and thanksgiving.

I also dedicate this book to my husband, Jason, who stood with me through every dashed hope, every failed IUI and IVF, through seven miscarriages, and through nearly four long, hard years trying to adopt. Without you, my love, I would have surely drowned in my own tears and sorrow. Without you, I would've given up many times. Your willingness to undergo fourteen years of hardship alongside me was such a gift and a blessing to me! You have been my rock—always.

To the many friends and family members who encouraged me to do this project. Without your kind words and without your encouragement, I probably would not have written this book.

Finally, to my content editor, Beth Graybill. Thank you for your kindness and your talent in helping me to focus in on the story and not get lost in the dizzying details. Thank you for pulling my story together to adequately tell God's story succinctly. Thank you to my graphic designer, Kayleigh McCann, to my friend, and proof editor, Jill Jones, and my photographer Erica Richard Photography

Thank you.

PREFACE

This book is written out of my heart and my desire to show God's faithfulness and sovereignty. My heart is to encourage people facing struggles of any kind. Although we face struggles in this life, that does not mean God is not right there, by our side, holding our hand. Sometimes He's even carrying us through the trials. He is so faithful to us. His love for us is far beyond anything we can comprehend and I want to encourage you to hold on.

Part One of this book is the journey of our infertility struggles. Part Two is the journey of our adoption process. Most of our adoption journey is pulled from my blog posts, as they most adequately convey the story and emotions as the events unfolded. These blog posts made way for this book, with the encouragement of many friends and family members.

PART ONE

INFERTILITY

CHAPTER 1

WHERE DO YOU SEE
THIS GOING?

Love at first sight. Okay, maybe not first sight, but pretty darn close.
I knew it. I knew Jason was "the one." Now I just had to wait for him
to know it. It took only two weeks for me to profess my love and
declare, "I already know we will be married someday. I know you're
the man I'm going to marry." Sure, he may have stood there in shock,
but I was not moved by that. I knew it. In fact, so did his father.

His father is a stoic man. One Sunday afternoon at church, while
I was sitting three rows ahead of him and his family, Jason's father
pointed me out to his wife and Jason's brother and made his own dec-
laration. He stated, very matter-of-factly, "Do you see that young lady
up there, the one with the blonde hair? Jason's going to marry her
someday."

Yes, he said it . . . three months before any of us even met. I had
just moved to Maine from Louisiana. I was new in town and new at

the church. No one knew me. But that day, my soon-to-be father-in-law declared that I would someday marry his son.

Fast forward three months. A woman I didn't know walked up to me abruptly and eagerly at church one Sunday. She introduced herself by name and asked if I'd come back to where she was sitting. Cautiously I agreed (stranger-danger was racing through my mind, but we were in church after all). I followed her to the back and she introduced me to her son, Jason.

"Jason, this is Bethanee. Bethanee, this is Jason. Bethanee, what's your phone number?"

As if in a trance, I rattled off my number. I think I was in shock. I don't normally make a habit of handing out my number to random strangers. However, this day I did. She *was* a kind and likeable woman after all, right? Awkward. Now what? I politely shook Jason's hand, smiled, timidly laughed, then excused myself back to my seat. That was the awkward introduction.

A few days later, on Christmas Eve of 1996 during the evening church service, Jason walked up to me and reintroduced himself. He shook my hand and apologized for the awkward beginning we had a few weeks earlier. This was the first time we spoke to one another without the awkward (but thankful) introduction of a parent.

Not long after that, we began talking on the phone and commuting to college together. We had a lot of late-night conversations—discussing everything from family to politics to education, and so much more. We discovered that we both longed to marry a person who wanted a large family, and also wanted to adopt. Jason and I both come from small families, and we both longed for additional siblings, including the camaraderie and the chaos. My extended family is very large so I had experienced what that felt like as a kid, and I wanted that for my own future family too. Jason's family was small, and he felt the same way. Neither of us had been exposed to adoption in our families and had no reason to long for the idea. But, as we discovered, we both independently longed to be adoptive parents. God was already beginning to paint a beautiful picture for our future lives—a picture we had no idea was in the works.

We officially began dating on a very romantic ice cream date that went something like this:

Jason: "Bethanee, where do you see this going?"

Me: "Well, hopefully someday we can begin dating."

Jason: "Okay, great. It's done."

I kid you not, that's how it happened! That should've been my very first clue that we would have a very logical romance.

The length of time we dated and were engaged was short—eleven months to be exact. Eleven months from the time we started dating to our walk down the aisle. We liked it that way. However, because our engagement was so short, there were a few rumors that we might be expecting our first child despite our public faith commitment to purity. But we were not expecting; we had stayed true to our commitment to God and each other.

When we got married and told our family and friends we planned to wait five years before trying to have children, most were surprised. But we had college to finish, lives to start, and a lot to do before we entered into that phase of our lives. Little did we know what a very long road we had ahead of us.

CHAPTER 2

Honey, Can We Have a Baby?

Two and a half years into our marriage I began to ask, "Honey, can we have a baby?" Jason was now working on his master's degree in electrical engineering, and he was busy. I was alone much of the time. But there it was, nagging at me. Begging me to ask him, "Honeeeeeey, can we have a baby?"

The answer was a firm "not yet." In his defense, Jason wanted to finish his degree so he could be a more present father. But, "Maybe we could start trying in a year.", he said. He would be very close to finishing his master's, and we both thought we could handle the strain it might put on our family. So, about a year later, we began trying for a baby with great excitement and expectation.

Little did we know the journey we were embarking on.

As a child, I used to pretend I was pregnant, nursing my baby and raising infants, practicing on my baby dolls. This was one of my dreams, to be a mom. I had other dreams, too. I wanted to be the CEO of a Fortune 500 company, and I wanted to travel the world. I wanted to major in international affairs even though I wasn't quite sure what international affairs meant as a kid (but it had the word "international" in it, so I wanted it). However, I always knew at the core of my being that I wanted to be a mom. I loved my mom. She was a great mom and I looked up to her. And, I loved kids.

After trying to get pregnant for many months without success, I finally went to see a fertility specialist. He ran through the standard protocol—timed intercourse, basal body temperature, charting my menstrual cycle, etc.—all to no avail. This was annoying to me because I had already researched and tried these things. Now I had to do them under the watchful eye of a fertility specialist, as if I didn't know what I was doing on my own.

Helpful Hint: If you're in the same place—trying to get pregnant with no success—take meticulous notes at home. Then bring them all in on that first visit so you can show the doctor everything you've done and he can evaluate your charts. This will likely move you further along in the process.

After trying the charting method, we moved on to Clomid (an infertility medication), and I noticed something very strange with one menstrual cycle in particular. Without going into detail, my "cycle" lasted longer than expected with a very strange tissue-like discharge. I called the doctor and he instructed me to take a break for a cycle when that cycle was done. He didn't really explain why, but I had a suspicion he knew the reason. Two months later, we began a new round of Clomid and more charting. This time we had a confirmed pregnancy. We were finally pregnant!

There I was, with a positive home pregnancy test and a positive blood test to prove it. It was as official as it could be. The excitement was tangible. But I didn't tell anyone. I wanted to tell my parents in a special way.

Days turned into weeks. We were waiting to go up to my parents' house in Maine to tell them. Then one day something strange began to happen, much like what had happened about three months prior. My menstrual cycle started, but something was different. This was not normal. A quick search on the Internet and I realized I was losing my baby. I called the doctor right away and gave my symptoms and as much information as I could. He told me I was likely losing the baby and wanted me to come in for a blood test and an ultrasound. Once I arrived at the doctor's office, they ran tests and confirmed what my heart already knew:

I was losing the baby.

I was crushed. I had never given miscarriage a thought. Not once had I ever contemplated that would happen to me, that I would be one of the statistics. But it was happening. My doctor and I discussed my unusual menstrual cycle three months prior and we both agreed I had lost a baby then too. That baby would've been around four to five weeks' gestation and this one was around seven weeks. With the knowledge of my two miscarriages, the doctor discussed my diet, environment, and overall health. At the time, I worked at a textile company. I was in the front office, but there were very strong, toxic chemicals being used on a daily basis all throughout the facility. The doctor suggested I leave that job and find a new one. I took his words to heart and gave my resignation the next day.

On the drive home from the doctor's appointment I felt numb. A sadness had come over me like I had never before experienced. I had to tell my husband that my body failed and the baby died. I felt tremendous shame and guilt because my body was, once again, the culprit of a new struggle in our family—two babies lost. I cried all the way home. I cried going to bed that night. I cried waking up the next morning. I leaned into God. He was the only one who could comfort me in the way I needed. And I leaned into these two verses:

> *"For as we share abundantly in Christ's sufferings, so through Christ we share abundantly in comfort too"*
>
> 1 CORINTHIANS 1:5 ESV

> *"God is our refuge and strength, a very present help in trouble"*
>
> PSALM 46:1 ESV

The doctor instructed us to wait two to three months before trying to conceive again. That was hard because it had already been fourteen months since we started trying for a baby, but we were going to try to adhere to his instructions. Honestly, in my mind I thought it didn't really matter anyway because we were having difficulty getting pregnant.

The following month we were just a married couple enjoying married sex. No charting. No drugs. No basal body temperature readings. Just good old married sex! Four weeks later, my menstrual cycle didn't start. I waited a few more days and it still hadn't started. One day, while I was out running errands, I picked up a pregnancy test. I nervously took the test at home while my husband was at work. The instructions essentially tell you to walk away and come back three minutes later to see your results, but I couldn't walk away. I just stood there and stared at the stick. My heart was in my throat. My mind was racing with negative thoughts of miscarriages, letting my husband down again, my body failing, and more hurt. I wanted the test to be positive, but I also didn't want to walk down the road of miscarriage again. Three minutes passed and there it was—the test was positive!

Wow! I was pregnant again. I didn't know what reaction to have so I stood there emotionless. I didn't cry. I wasn't happy (well, I was, but I was afraid to be happy). I didn't call Jason. I just stood there, afraid. Finally I came to my senses and called the doctor's office. They asked me to come right into the office for a blood test. I was afraid to because we weren't supposed to have gotten pregnant that month, as per the doctor's orders. But I went in, and he was cautiously happy for me. They drew some blood and sent me home. I had to wait four hours for the results of the blood test. Finally, after what seemed like an eternity, a call came in from the office and confirmed that I was, in fact, pregnant!

Fast forward thirty-five weeks and our first little baby boy was born. We named him Caleb Michael. He was premature but doing well. I was actually the one not doing well. I had developed pre-ec-lampsia and then HELLPS. After a week's stay in the hospital—and a fierce allergic reaction to the magnesium sulfate I was being given to help my body not have seizures and fight HELLPS—we were both released.

If you're curious about the medical explanations (what I call *The MEs*) for what we went through but need to hear them in layman's terms, then these sections are for you.

The ME: HELLP Syndrome is a life-threatening pregnancy complication, usually considered to be a sign or complication of pre-eclampsia. Both conditions usually occur in the later stages of pregnancy, or sometimes after childbirth. HELLP is an abbreviation of the three main features of the syndrome: Hemolysis, Elevated Liver enzymes, and Low Platelet count.

Source: wikipedia

CHAPTER 3

WHAT ARE YOUR PLANS?

When our son, Caleb, was four months old, my husband and I gave ourselves the green light to start trying for another baby.

Going through infertility gave us a different perspective on trying to conceive. Questions like "When should we start trying for another child?" became harder to answer. With uncertainty as to how long it would take to conceive again, we had to guesstimate when considering the approximate distance we wanted our children separated in age. I told Jason we could start trying as soon as I could handle the news without crying—simply from the sleep-deprived state of mind we were in with a newborn in the house.

So, since Caleb had been sleeping through the night since he was eight weeks old, at four months we felt normal again. Thinking it would take another fourteen months or so to conceive, we hoped this would put the kids roughly two years apart.

With that, we started the process on our own. One month passed, two months, three . . . . When my cycle was late that third month I dipped into my home stash of pregnancy tests and tested again while Jason was at work. Three minutes later I saw two lines!

We were expecting.

The shock ran through me as I calculated the due date and realized the two babies would be just fifteen months apart. All I could think at first was, *Wow, fifteen months apart. That's really close!* Thoughts of miscarriages bounced around in my head. But this felt different. Probably because we did not have to go through any infertility treatments. Maybe that gave me a false sense of security, but I was not nervous like I had been with my pregnancy with Caleb.

I did some quick planning that day. I made a fancy candle-lit dinner, grabbed a bottle of wine (for Jason), and hand-stamped a card that read, *"What are your plans on April 19, 2002?"* On the inside the card read, *"Becoming a dad to your newborn son or daughter."* We both celebrated that night, especially when we realized our infertility issues must be over. This one was so easy. No doctors. No meds. No crying, longing, waiting, or expecting. It was just like it was supposed to be. Normal.

Not a single thing went wrong with this pregnancy, and nine months later the sweetest and prettiest little girl, with two huge dimples and a head full of golden-blonde hair, was born. Our little Tiera-Belle was safely with us. We rejoiced!

CHAPTER 4

SOMEWHERE IN THE MIDDLE OF IRELAND

Life was full and busy. What I didn't mention in the last chapter was that our son, Caleb, was delayed in most activities and motor skills due to his premature birth at thirty-five weeks. From birth through roughly six months, he was mostly paralyzed on his left side. We spent a lot of time at Boston Children's Hospital trying to determine if Caleb had had a stroke in utero or if it was something else. I spent two to three days a week with him in physical therapy, occupational therapy, and speech therapy. Meanwhile, our daughter, Tiera, was on the fast track with all of her motor skills. Because of Caleb's therapies and the fact that we had two babies under the age of two, we decided to wait to expand our family again. We welcomed the break and were feeling confident that whatever caused the fertility problems in the beginning would no longer be an issue.

Boy were we wrong.

After about a year we decided it was time to grow our little family again, we started the same way we had always started: naturally. After several months of trying, there was no pregnancy so I contacted our fertility specialist. After a brief check-up, he prescribed another round of Clomid—the medicine used to induce ovulation. We tried several months of timed intercourse while using the Clomid, with no results. We were so disappointed

The ME: If you're new to this journey or walking alongside someone who is struggling with infertility, here's how this works with the female reproductive system.

Each month, a follicle in the ovary develops a single mature egg (unless you struggle with PCOS—polycystic ovarian syndrome). That mature egg is released from the ovarian follicle—on either the right side or the left—and travels to the uterus where the egg can be fertilized by the sperm. But because I only had *one* fallopian tube open for the eggs to travel from the ovary to the uterus, that meant I was fertile only *every other month.* So, every other month, my left ovary released an egg that was blocked by a knot in my left fallopian tube. On those months, the egg and the sperm could never get to each other, so eventually the egg and the sperm would die and be absorbed by my body.

The HSG Test, or Hysterosalpingogram Test, was how I discovered that my left fallopian tube was tied in a knot. This test pushes dye through the vagina into the uterus and the fallopian tubes. This way, the ultrasound technician and fertility specialist can track the flow of the dye to determine if there are any blockages with the flow. If there are no blockages, the

> dye will flow directly into the abdominal cavity. If there are blockages, they will immediately appear on the ultrasound screen. And that's what happened with me.

The specialist decided to run further medical tests on us. For Jason, they ran a sperm count test. Thankfully the test showed that absolutely nothing was wrong with him. Then they ran tests on me to determine if my reproductive system was functioning as it was supposed to be. The results of my test showed that my left fallopian tube was tied—literally tied in a knot. I did some research and couldn't find any information on it within the medical community, but that was what was happening. This was my issue.

That was very disappointing news. However, there were documented cases of women who got pregnant fairly quickly after an HSG test because the dye cleared blockages during the test. And even better news—the knotted fallopian tube was a fairly easy fix with a quick laparoscopic procedure.

Several days later, Jason drove me to the outpatient surgery unit at the hospital where I underwent the procedure. It was a simple surgery with three very small incisions in my abdomen. The problem for me: I have bladder anxiety (yes, this is a real diagnosis!). When I sensed external pressure to urinate (i.e., doctors and nurses telling me I had to pee before I could go home from the hospital) or there was a possibility that someone was standing near the bathroom door and could hear me pee, I just couldn't release the urine, no matter how badly I had to go. The nurses and doctors were pumping a ton of fluids into me to force my body to respond, and Jason was begging me to drink more so we could go home to our kids. Just one time . . . that's all they needed from me. But this bladder anxiety was no joke and I just couldn't force myself to pee.

By 9:30 p.m. we were tired and frustrated. I had been out of surgery for hours and still, no matter how much I drank or sat on the toilet, I just couldn't convince my bladder to relax. I wanted to leave that hospital! I wanted to be home with my babies! But I was being held a prisoner by my own anxious bladder and the hospital staff who wanted to make sure I was okay. Finally, Jason got a huge pitcher of tap water and—with a fun spirit to lighten my grumpy mood—made me guzzle the whole pitcher. Within minutes of guzzling, I started screaming at Jason to grab a throw-up bin. He got it positioned just in time for me to throw up all of the liquids I had drunk that day. (I have an aversion to lukewarm water to this day!). But I never did pee.

By 10:00 p.m. we were begging the doctors to allow us to go home. As all good doctors and nurses should, they explained the risks of going home without knowing if my bladder was going to be okay. They told us we could leave if we promised to return to the hospital emergency room if I had not urinated by midnight. We were anxious to get home to our kids, so we agreed to these terms. Before we even made it home, I had to go to the bathroom. Praise God! Thankfully, I managed to hold off all those fluids until I reached our house. But I have never in my life run so fast to my own bathroom as I did that night. And it was a good feeling knowing that no damage had been done to my bladder during the surgery.

With that procedure behind us, I now had a new hope that we would be able to get pregnant more easily. Between the HSG test and the laparoscopic surgery, I thought we were on the fast track to getting pregnant.

Now, maybe it's just my type-A personality, but infertility was so very discouraging and difficult! I saw every month without a positive pregnancy test as a lost month. Every passing month was another *two-week-wait* (2WW) to endure.

> *The ME:* The Two-Week-Wait (2WW) is the two weeks between ovulation and menstruation. This is the time when a couple has to simply wait to see if the sperm fertilized the egg and conceived a baby.

Never has two weeks felt so long as the two weeks waiting to discover if *that* month was the successful month. The 2WW is painful and emotionally taxing, or at least it was for me. I scrutinized every twinge, every heightened smell surrounding me, every sore-breast-moment, and every abnormal craving. I longed to hear the good news from that little pee-stick, "You're pregnant!" But it never came. Month after month, my hopes and dreams of more children and a larger family were dashed.

Infertility becomes particularly hard if you *already* have children. Why? Because of these two reasons:

1. You know that you're missing out on more love and more of the unbreakable bond that comes between a parent and a child.
2. People begin to judge you because you're frustrated by infertility when you already have children. It's as if everyone thinks you should just give up and be grateful.

For some, this last reason may be a valid argument, but not for Jason and me. Infertility after two children felt nearly as hard to handle as the failed attempts at growing our family in the very beginning. We heard comments like

"Well, at least you have two healthy kids."

"Why don't you just stop?"

"Why do you keep doing this? You have two kids already and many people can't have any kids. Be happy you at least have that."

While those may be true statements, they did not negate the fact that Jason and I had dreamt of a large family. We dreamt of the pitter-patter or *many* little feet running throughout our home. We dreamt of the noise and the chaos. And, even stronger than those feelings, we both clearly sensed God was calling us to have a large family. Why were people judging our choices and our intentions? We just didn't understand.

****

*If this is YOU, then here's my **Helpful Hint:***

There will be people in your life who will not understand your infertility journey, no matter how hard you try to explain your thoughts, your feelings, your calling, your choices. They just simply cannot understand. And I want to encourage you that it is not the business of other people to tell you how to run your family. It is not the business of others to interject their opinions into whether you should have more children or not. It is not the business of other people to throw up their disapproval of your desires all over you. And furthermore, it is no one else's place to judge what you sense God has called you and your family to do. I learned this the hard way throughout our many years of struggle.

Also know this—people will say the words they believe to be most helpful and kind. They will try to say these things to you out of love. People will mean well but say awkward things out of their own discomfort with your situation or due to their inability to effectively communicate the hurt and sadness they feel for you. They may accidentally hurt you when what they really want is to help you. Say to these people, "I know you're trying to help, but it's actually hurting my feelings and making me feel more sad. I would appreciate your positive encouragement and your prayers."

And if this is SOMEONE YOU LOVE, then here's my Helpful Hint:

If you are the one struggling to find the right words to say to your daughter, your sister, your niece, or dear friend, then I would encourage you to offer a hug, a shoulder to cry on, and a simple prayer, again and again.

You may want to encourage them or fix their situation with the right words or reminders, but often this kind of response is not helpful. It just pours salt into already open and raw wounds of the heart and mind. They just need to know that you are there for them, without judgment, without solutions, without shame. Sit and listen to them, pray for them, bring them a meal, let them cry on your shoulder. I would've wanted to hear, "I'm sorry you're going through all of this! I am praying for you. How else can I support you?"

****

At this point, our fertility specialist was recommending further action and more drastic measures. So, we began our first cycle of ovulation stimulants that I had to inject nightly into a one-inch area around my belly button.

I remember the first time I had to inject that needle into myself. I counted to three then pulled my hand back and got ready to stab my abdomen with the tiny needle. I paused with my hand raised, needle in the air. Thoughts flashed through my mind. I wondered if this was going to be worth it—if it would hurt as much as I anticipated, if I had the courage to stab myself with a needle. Then, just as quickly as those thoughts came and went, I lowered my hand and jabbed the needle into my abdomen.

"Okay, that wasn't nearly as bad as I thought it was going to be. I think I can do this!" And just like that, I became a pro.

We did this month after month, cycle after cycle, but nothing happened. I injected myself with ovulation stimulants night after night—hoping and praying that this would be "the month." So many tears were shed and so much praying was done. God was so faithful in those times and I knew I could continue trusting Him, but the sadness grew heavier with each passing month.

During this time, God was really showing me how to draw near to Him. He brought Jeremiah 29:13–14 (NIV) to mind, which says, *You will seek me and find me when you seek me with all your heart. I will be found by you," declares the Lord.*

This was my anchor: knowing that I will find God every single time I seek Him. In all the struggles and hardships, I will find God if I daily get on my knees and seek Him. And He promises that we will find Him. God does not promise to take away our problems or give us a struggle-free life, but He promises to be found and to be present with us. Hallelujah. That gave me such hope.

Finally, the day came. The 2WW ended and it was time for me to go in for my normal 6:00 a.m. blood draw routine. The nurse drew my blood, and within seconds I was on my way home to wait for a phone call with the results. Once home, I took a home pregnancy test (I was now obsessed with peeing on a stick at least once a day!) and I waited for my own results too. I thought I could see a faint line . . . but was it "hope" or was there really a line on that stick? I wasn't sure. I held that stick under a lamp, up to the bathroom light; I even took it to the back deck to see it in daylight. I twisted and turned it every single way possible, hoping I would see a hint of a line. If you are no stranger to infertility you are likely no stranger to this odd behavior.

I waited impatiently for a phone call from the doctor's office. Finally they called with great news: *we were expecting!*

I breathed a sigh of relief! One large hurdle was overcome. Now we had another large hurdle to overcome: could I carry this baby to term? I had already had two miscarriages, but the doctors didn't seem nearly as concerned as I was. I was instructed to pick up some pro-gesterone cream, so I quickly hopped in my car, ran to the pharmacy, and did exactly what the doctors told me to do. We waited with bated breath as our days turned into weeks. The little life inside of me grew to have a heartbeat and the tiniest little arms and legs. Such a joy to see movement and life!

One afternoon I was sitting on the couch. The house was quiet. I was resting while the kids were taking a nap. At that point, I was nine weeks pregnant and things had been going well. As I sat there that day, however, I felt fluid begin to gush out of me. I ran to the bathroom where I saw a horrible sight—blood, and a lot of it. I immediately ran to the phone and called my fertility specialist, who told me to come in right away. The staff knew us well so they warmly greeted me. I could tell they were worried for us too. I was reassured that blood flow during pregnancy can happen and it did not necessarily mean a miscarriage.

They got me into the ultrasound room immediately to check on our little peanut. The monitor was turned away from me—which I discovered was typical protocol for a possible miscarriage. Maybe they wanted to protect me, maybe they didn't want to have to answer a million questions while trying to do their job, but I just remember it being a painful part of my experience. I wanted to see my child. I wanted to see the child I had been longing for and praying for for so long. *My child.* All I wanted was to see what they were seeing on that monitor too.

Finally, after a dreadful wait, the doctors shared that our baby had died and my body was trying to flush out all remnants of the baby. I wanted to scream. I would have given my own life to preserve the life that was in me. *This wasn't my plan!* This wasn't my dream, but there was nothing I could do. The doctors sent me home with instructions to return in forty-eight hours for ultrasounds and more blood work. There were more instructions but I tried to block them from my mind. It was too much for me. I was a mess. I felt so alone. So very alone.

I could hear nothing that day. I walked out to my car numb, bleeding, crying, and alone. I was angry. I wanted answers. Why was my body having such a hard time maintaining a pregnancy? Why couldn't I carry these precious little ones to full-term? Were these all babies that had genetic defects and my body knew that and therefore was miscarrying them automatically? Was this my body's inability to produce a good enough uterine lining for the embryos to attach to? Was it my body's inability to produce enough natural progesterone to sustain a pregnancy, once a pregnancy was detected? Or was it something else?

Thus began another battery of tests for Jason and me. As it turns out, the tests didn't reveal a solid reason for the miscarriages. We talked about the discovery during one of my caesarean sections that my uterine wall was extremely thin. This muscle is supposed to be fairly thick and strong, but mine was like tissue paper. In fact, I remember the labor and delivery doctors telling me that I should not attempt a natural delivery in any subsequent pregnancies and that I should deliver by thirty-seven weeks (instead of the full-term forty weeks) in order to avoid a ruptured uterus. The infertility doctors questioned if my thin uterine wall could be an issue, but they had no concrete medical evidence that it could cause recurrent miscarriages.

With no answers but a strong calling from God to keep going, we did just that—we kept going. We took a three-month break, then started back up with infertility treatments. This time our doctor recommended Intra-Uterine Insemination, otherwise known as IUI or Artificial Insemination.

Our everyday lives were consumed with more abdominal shots and new drugs, 6:00 a.m. blood draws at the lab (which also meant unpredictable early morning traffic with sleepy kids in the car), ultrasounds, and finally the 2WW. Month after month, we repeated this process with no results. The new medicine would carry my body all the way to the point of being ready to ovulate. At that point I would inject myself with HSG, the ovulation stimulant that forces the follicles to rupture open, and then we would wait a couple of days before Jason and I could go into the doctor's office for the actual IUI procedure.

During this time of IUI attempts, my journal entries were filled with prayers asking God for each cycle to work and then to stick. My heart ached for a positive pregnancy test followed by a full-term healthy pregnancy. I kept reading over the words of Lamentations 3:25, *"The Lord is good to those who wait for him, to the soul who seeks him" (ESV).*

A few months passed and we were wrapping up another 2WW. I had no symptoms and my daily home-pregnancy-test routine was not yielding positive results either. It was time for my 6:00 a.m. blood draw at the lab. I checked in at the front desk, walked back for my one-minute procedure, then hopped in my car and drove all the way back home. I walked in the door and went back to bed. Around 10:00 a.m. the lab called with my results. This was the phone call I had been waiting for all morning. They said we were expecting! I was in shock because I had not expected the IUI to work this month. I had been tracking and had no symptoms at all. None. So, that began to worry me.

All I could think about was, *Why don't I have symptoms? Does that mean this pregnancy is doomed from the very beginning?*

The questions were relentless at first, but then I realized, as I had come to realize many times prior, that God was in control and I just needed to trust Him. There was little to nothing I could do to preserve this pregnancy on my own. When I was seven weeks pregnant, I went in for an ultrasound. We could see our little nugget. The ultrasound revealed tiny arms and legs were forming and picked up on the faintest heartbeat. My breasts were now sore and swollen. Fatigue was setting in. *Symptoms!* They were welcomed guests in my book.

A few days after that ultrasound, Jason and I left for a much-needed vacation and break in Ireland. We had been planning this trip for quite some time and we were both really looking forward to our time away together. Since I was now beginning to have some signs of pregnancy (especially fatigue), taking a red-eye flight across the Atlantic when I was exhausted and couldn't sleep sitting up wasn't so brilliant on our part. But we didn't know I would be at this stage in a pregnancy when we booked the tickets. Awake for almost twenty-four hours during the first leg of our trip, all I wanted to do was close my eyes and get some sleep! But that would not happen for a few more hours.

We landed in London around 8:00 a.m., a little later than expected. As the plane was landing, one of the flight attendants announced over the speaker, "When we land, we do not want anyone to get up out of their seats. We have two guests who need to reach a connecting flight immediately once we land. The plane is at the gate and ready to leave, waiting for them to board. Would Jason and Bethanee Syversen please raise your hands so we can come speak to you?"

Oh my word! This could not be good. The plane was so late that our connecting flight to Dublin was fully boarded and waiting on us. If you've ever flown into London, you know it's not a small airport. The plane landed, and Jason and I were escorted off the plane and immediately told where to go. We sprinted for the gate where our connecting flight was waiting for us. We sprinted for several long minutes with some of our luggage in tow to our new gate, which must have been all the way across Heathrow Airport. We barely made it in time. We rushed down the gate ramp, winded, adrenaline coursing through our veins. Everyone waiting on the plane stared at us as we found our seats. I was absolutely exhausted.

A couple of hours later we were in Dublin. We found our way to our first bed-and-breakfast. Ireland was gorgeous! There was so much rich history there and so much beauty, from the countryside to the tombs to the Cliffs of Moher. It still ranks as one of our all-time favorite trips. Jason and I love our vacations together because we don't follow guided tours or the popular tourist sites and attractions. We rent a car and travel the back country roads—our usual way to travel in whatever country we visit. This is how we really get to see the unique culture and meet many locals. We also stay at bed-and-breakfasts rather than hotels for much the same reason.

Several days into our trip to Ireland, we were staying way off the beaten path at a very quaint bed-and-breakfast deep in the countryside. It was nearing bedtime so Jason and I were settling into our room for the evening. I used the restroom and discovered that I had begun to bleed. With sadness, I hollered out to Jason, "I think I'm miscarrying again."

My heart was breaking. My mind raced with thoughts about the trip sprinting through Heathrow Airport in London, and I couldn't help but wonder if all the running and carrying heavy bags over my shoulders had caused my body to miscarry. The reality was that my body struggled to carry pregnancies to term regardless, so sprinting through Heathrow was probably not the cause, but it was the only reason I could think of.

The bleeding continued throughout the night, and eventually the heavy cramps came too. Jason went downstairs to the front desk and asked the evening host for something that might help with the pain. The sweet host came up with a heating pad filled with hot water. I laid that over my abdomen and started to cry. This wasn't how the trip was supposed to go. More importantly, it wasn't how the pregnancy was supposed to go. I was heartbroken.

Jason prayed with me throughout that night. Together, we decided we would still try to enjoy the remainder of our time in Ireland. But I continued to miscarry our baby throughout the rest of the trip so it was hard to enjoy much of anything. Even to this day, when I look at our pictures of Ireland, I have very mixed emotions. I treasure the memories we made seeing so many beautiful places and the time we had together. But as I look at the pictures of me from the first part of the trip, I'm reminded I was carrying a child in those pictures . . . and in the last pictures from our trip, my body was processing the remains of our child and expelling them like an unwanted mass of "cells." That was my baby, and he or she was loved and wanted.

"Truly, truly, I say to you, you will weep and lament, but the world will rejoice. You will be sorrowful, but your sorrow will turn into joy. When a woman is giving birth, she has sorrow because her hour has come, but when she has delivered the baby, she no longer remembers the anguish, for joy that a human being has been born into the world. So also you have sorrow now, but I will see you again, and your hearts will rejoice, and no one will take your joy from you."

John 16:20–22 ESV

****

My husband is an engineer, which translates to a very analytical, logical approach to processing emotions, for him at least. He could intellectually process this miscarriage, and the ones before, without expressing much emotion. I was the opposite. So, when it came to processing these events together, it was always hard on me. I was emotional and expressive. I wanted answers as to WHY. *Why can't my body do this? Why is my body failing me? Why do we keep miscarrying?* It was a very demoralizing time for me. I felt personally responsible for all of our troubles. It was my body failing me, failing *us*.

Jason didn't see it that way at all. He simply wanted logical answers. As an engineer, his brain is hardwired (and trained) to figure things out. He thinks, *There's a problem, so how can I reverse engineer it and reprogram it to function correctly?* He started to analyze our miscarriage "situation" from a medical perspective and a healthcare insurance perspective (or rather, his perspective on how the healthcare system is so broken and doesn't cover all the tests and procedures). This was his way of helping to ease my pain. I love him for that; however, what I really needed him to say in that moment was that he too was hurting. I needed to hear that he too longed to hold these little ones, and that it hurt him to not have answers as to why it was all happening. But I knew he cared.

*MEN: If by chance you're reading this book too, then this is my **Helpful Hint** for you:*

Men, be sympathetic to your wife's very fragile emotions during this time. Understand to the best of your ability how challenging this may be for her. Hug her. Hold her. Buy her a nice meal, bring it home, set up a candlelight dinner, and give her the opportunity to just talk through her emotions without trying to fix the problem. Then hug her again. After a few days have passed, don't assume she's okay. Don't assume since you haven't seen her cry that she's no longer thinking about it. She is. This child was in her body, consuming space, nutrients, blood, and most importantly, her heart, for however many weeks. It's not over for her. It's highly personal. Highly personal. In my brain, it was my body that continued to fail—not that I was a failure, but my body was failing me. Understand that, men. She needs you more than you think. A helpful place to start is by simply asking, "What's on your mind right now?" Then listen, without fixing, as she answers.

****

INFERTILITY: *the inability to conceive after one year of unpro-tected intercourse (six months if the woman is over age thirty-five) or the inability to carry a pregnancy to live birth.*

Did you know . . . ?

- Only 7.4 million women, or 11.9% of women, have received infertility services in their lifetime (2006–2010 National Survey of Family Growth, CDC).

31

- One in eight couples (or 12% of married women) have trouble getting pregnant or sustaining a pregnancy (2006–2010 National Survey of Family Growth, CDC).
- Approximately one-third of infertility cases are attributed to the female partner, one-third are attributed to the male partner, and one-third are caused by a combination of problems in both partners or is unexplained (www.asrm.org).
- Couples between the ages of 29 and 33 with a normal functioning reproductive system have only a 20–25% chance of conceiving in any given month (National Women's Health Resource Center).
- After six months of trying to get pregnant, 60% of couples will conceive without medical assistance (Infertility as a Covered Benefit, William M. Mercer Inc., 1997, a published study).
- Approximately 44% of women with infertility have sought medical assistance. Of those who seek medical intervention, approximately 65% give birth (Infertility as a Covered Benefit, William M. Mercer Inc., 1997, a published study).
- Approximately 85–90% of infertility cases are treated with drug therapy or surgical procedures. Fewer than 3% need advanced reproductive technologies such as in vitro fertilization (IVF) (www.asrm.org).
- The most recently available statistics indicate the live birth rate per fresh non-donor embryo transfer is 47.7% if the woman is under 35 years of age and 39.2% if the woman is age 35–37. (Society for Assisted Reproductive Technology, 2013)
- A study published in the *New England Journal of Medicine*

(August 2002) found that the percentage of high-order pregnancies (those with three or more fetuses) was greater in states that did not require insurance coverage for IVF. The authors of the study noted that mandatory coverage is likely to yield better health outcomes for women and their infants since high-order births are associated with higher-risk pregnancies.[1]

---

[1] www.resolve.org

CHAPTER 5

OUR CHRISTMAS MIRACLE

A few months after our trip to Ireland, the dust settled and we had some pillow-talk discussion about starting the Intra-Uterine Insemination, or IUI, process over again. We agreed we would start again soon, then prayed together. The next morning, we both woke up ready to tackle infertility again.

Starting the process over meant daily injections into my abdomen, 6:00 a.m. blood tests every few days, "special visits" to the infertility specialists (as I affectionately referred to the IUI days), and more 2WWs. This time around, we added more injections.

Not only was I doing ovulation stimulant injections into my abdomen during the first two weeks of my cycle, but now I was doing daily injections of progesterone into my hip during the last two weeks of my cycle. The progesterone was an added measure to try and tackle the recurrent miscarriages.

The doctors had to give me a short lesson on these new injections, but when they took the syringe and needle out of the package, I froze. The new needles were HUGE. If you haven't been through this, then let me tell you, it's intimidating! I just kept thinking, *This could not be what they want me to stab into myself. Not THAT needle. Or maybe that's just the practice needle so they have a larger model for those that can't see well.* But yes, that was the needle! It was an abnormal size, unlike any other needle I had ever seen before. I wasn't afraid of needles! I had my blood drawn frequently, donated blood at blood drives, and had been giving myself daily injections into my abdomen for quite some time. However, when I saw that progesterone needle, I knew I was afraid of *that* needle (18-gauge 1.5-inch monsters!). It was so large that I could see the hole going up the needle and see the contents coming down through the needle.

The day I got my first progesterone needle lesson was the day I actually needed to start the injections. I got home from the doctor's office knowing I would be injecting myself that night with that monstrosity. I couldn't imagine how, but I knew I had to. I had to give myself that progesterone due to the life that may have started growing in me that day. It would take the sheer willpower of a "wanna-be mother" to make me stab myself with that beast of a needle. Night came way too fast, and it was time. I asked my husband if he would do the injection for me, but he wasn't able to do it, so I pulled my pants just below my hip, wiped my skin clean with a rubbing alcohol wipe, waited for it to dry *(ladies, wait for it to dry! It will save you pain!)*, and filled the syringe with the progesterone oil. I pulled my arm back and . . . and thought, *I can't do this. I cannot do this.* More panic filled me. *How can I do this? I have to do this. Bethanee, you have to do this! This is for the life of a potential baby. You must! Just don't think about it. Just do it quickly—you've got this! I am woman, hear me roar!* Yes, I actually said that to myself inside my head.

I pulled my arm back again and held it in the injection position. I swung the needle toward my hip with gusto. Suddenly, I felt like I could hear brakes coming to a screeching halt in my head. I got about three centimeters from my skin and stopped. I just couldn't do it. The fear of the pain from that massive needle intimidated me. How does one prepare to inflict pain on oneself? That was a hard question for me. This may not have been an issue for other women, but I was struggling. I had to step away from it. I walked downstairs, talked with my husband, and watched a bit of TV with him. I had to relax.

An hour later I returned upstairs and decided I needed to do it this time. I mean, actually *do it*! I gave myself another pep talk and counted to three. I told myself that by the end of number three, that needle had to be in my hip, injecting the potentially life-saving progesterone oil into me. So, I counted: 1, 2, 3 . . . I swung my hand towards my hip with gusto again. Progress was made, but the needle still was not in. It had just barely broken my skin. A tiny drop of blood gathered at the puncture point and I looked down, wondering how I was going to make this happen. How could I get that huge needle all the way in so I could inject the oil? But being a determined and stubborn girl, I was not going to let this needle get the best of me. Now I had anger on my side. Without even giving it much thought, I launched my arm back, flung it forward with the greatest gusto yet, and jabbed it into my hip!

"It's in! It's all the way in! I did it! I did it!"

A sense of relief washed over me. As the oil slowly went in, I realized it didn't hurt at all. I didn't feel it at all. In fact, the abdominal injections were way more painful, and the abdominal needle was teeny tiny! I finished with the injection and I cleaned up. There were no side effects except for a small grape-sized lump under my skin that eventually dissipated as the oil dispersed throughout my body.

Success! As the nights went on I quickly became a pro at injecting progesterone and this became my new norm.

During my follow-up appointments, I inquired as to why the hip injections never hurt but the abdominal ones sometimes did, and even left bruises. The nurse told me that the hip is mostly a fatty part of your body and it carries very few nerves in it, whereas the belly button is loaded with many small nerves (abdominal injections happen within a one-inch radius around your belly button). It's very possible to hit a nerve when giving the abdominal injections, and when you do, it's more painful and leaves occasional bruises.

Months passed with no sign of life growing in me. This was such a long, hard journey. I wished so much to be off the emotional roller coaster of infertility. I wished to have a normal sex life with my husband. And I longed for normal conversations with my husband, friends, and family. Raising small children during this time was always interesting, too, because we were frequently having to take them to appointments with us or find sitters while the "special visits" were taking place. For the most part, though, they were unaware. They were little enough at this point that they didn't know if we were undergoing a procedure or were pregnant or losing a baby. We mostly shielded them from that stuff.

I was comforted by my daily devotional time with God. I was reminded by the apostle Paul in 2 Corinthians 4:8–9, *"We are hard pressed on every side, but not crushed; perplexed, but not in despair; persecuted, but not abandoned; struck down, but not destroyed" (NIV).* This wisdom gave me strength to keep going.

Another "special" IUI office visit came and went. As the 2WW progressed, the time for my pregnancy blood test came closer and closer. I began getting anxious, and the POAS (*pee-on-a-stick*) routine went into overdrive at home. I would POAS multiple times per day, hoping and praying I would see something.

On the morning I was to go into the lab for my blood test, I saw a solid line on the stick! I had previously read that progesterone could give false positives, so I didn't trust it. But I would be lying

Measure your life by loss and not by gain,
Not by the wine drunk but the wine poured forth.
For love's strength is found in love's sacrifice,
And he who suffers most has most to give.

Henry Ward Beecher

if I didn't tell you I was very hopeful because of that positive. After the 6:00 a.m. blood test, I did my usual—drove home and waited. I don't recall when the call came in, but when it did, I was so thrilled! We were finally expecting! I called my husband at work and told him the good news. He responded with a stoic, "That's good news. But I'm not going to get excited until we pass the first trimester." I was hurt. I wanted him to be happy! I understood mentally why he responded that way—he was protecting us. But we were pregnant and we had new progesterone weapons in our arsenal. That was going to make the difference, I just knew it.

I went in for my first ultrasound at six weeks. I saw our Little Bean and a six-week-old heartbeat. I was beaming. The doctor measured the baby and gave me an estimated due date. I was hopeful. Because of all the miscarriages I had experienced to date, my doctors were overly cautious and scheduled me for internal ultrasounds often. That made me very happy. It left no room for guessing if the baby was still alive and doing well. Weeks seven, eight, nine, and ten passed. All measurements and ultrasounds were right on track. I remember the moment I realized I was close to getting out of the first trimester. I was so close to being able to breathe a sigh of relief.

I went in for another ultrasound at eleven weeks and everything looked amazing. Our Little Bean was on target for all measurements and everything else. I left happier than I had been in a long time. We had made it past a huge milestone! Never before had I miscarried beyond this point with any of my previous pregnancies and I was feeling confident.

A couple of days later, I felt the gush.

I don't even remember what I was doing—I think I blocked it out. There is no "normal gushing" in pregnancy, not mine at least. I fell to the ground and just began to weep. I didn't need a doctor to tell me what I already knew—our Little Bean was gone. In the blink of an eye, Little Bean was dashed from my future. This sweet little life would never be held and would never get to experience the love of their big brother and big sister who longed to hold them. I lay on the floor, weeping uncontrollably. I just could not believe I was experiencing such loss. I couldn't believe this was happening *again*—for the *fifth time.* I knew people who had had *a* miscarriage, maybe two at the most. But I felt I was in a league of my own at this point. I knew no one who had experienced this kind of loss.

I eventually gathered my emotions, scraped myself off the floor, and called my doctor, then called Jason. Jason was at a loss for words. He wanted to help but what could he say? This was his baby too and he was experiencing loss in his own way . . . and he was having to do it at work. It was quiet on the phone.

My doctor asked me to meet him at the hospital in the morning.

Jason came with me this time. He wanted to see the ultrasound. He wanted to yell at the doctor and ask, "WHY? Why is this happening? Why can't you guys stop it? Why aren't you doing anything?" He wanted to fix it—all of it—but he couldn't. The doctors couldn't fix it either.

They were trying, but so far, the best they had come up with was "unexplained infertility with unexplained recurrent miscarriages." That was not an acceptable answer for him, or for me, but there was nothing we could do about it. I was still bleeding and cramping a great deal when we arrived at the hospital that morning. They did the ultrasound and determined that Little Bean had moved onto heaven— though they would never actually say it that way. It was decided that the best thing to do was a D&C (dilation & curettage) surgical procedure. Our Little Bean was still in one piece, and delivering the baby could take a long time and could be hard, so they wanted to do this procedure.

I wish now I had known better. I wish I had fought to deliver Little Bean instead of going through with the D&C. I wish I could have held Little Bean and told Little Bean how much he or she meant to me. I wish I had known that a D&C was the same procedure used for abortions, and to the hospital staff, this was merely an abortion. But this was no abortion. This was my child! This was the child that had been longed for, hoped for, and prayed for, for a very long time! I wish I had used my voice to say no. A D&C was not medically necessary for me at that point.

The hospital staff helped me into a hospital gown. I was hoisted up onto a gurney where I was instructed to lie down and was hooked up to an IV. I remember Jason standing by my side, holding my hand, whispering words of love and encouragement to me, and praying

41

for me. His wife, the one he promised to always love and protect, he couldn't protect from this. He couldn't make all the pain, physical or emotional, go away.

It was time for the D&C. I remember the nurses coming to get me. And I remember crying as I left Jason's side. I just wanted him there. I needed him there. I was so afraid, not of the procedure but of the emotional turmoil in my mind. I needed stability and he was the most tangible, stable thing I had. I prayed silently. I begged God for the results to be different. I begged Him to save my baby and to take away the pain, but that didn't happen. Yet never, through all of this, did I believe God had done this to me. I knew this was the consequence of living in a fallen world with a broken body. The God I knew was the same God of Deuteronomy 7:9, *"Know therefore that the Lord your God is God, the faithful God who keeps covenant and steadfast love with those who love him and keep his commandments, to a thousand generations" (ESV).*

I went into that operating room clinging to that reminder.

The doctor walked in, examined me in a rather violating way (To this day, when I think about this it still brings me to tears. Years later I discovered this fertility clinic had been taken to court and sued for many sexual assault violations toward women while under anesthesia.), spoke to the nurse, never addressed me, and walked away. Moments later I was in surgery, and finally transferred to the recovery room. Once in the recovery room, the nurses came in and asked me if I'd like genetic testing done on the remains of Little Bean. Without hesitating, I said yes. I needed answers. I wanted answers. *Were my babies all dying because we were creating children with severe genetic disabilities so serious they were not even able to make it in my womb? Or were my babies healthy?* I needed to know—no matter what the answer was. This answer would help us determine if we were going to keep trying to conceive.

Jason waited for me to fully recover, staying by my side the whole time we were at the hospital. I shed a lot of tears in those hours waiting to be cleared to go home. We were finally released. The drive home was long and mostly silent. I couldn't say anything without instantly crying. My baby had died, a doctor had treated me in a way that felt violating, and they had taken my baby from my womb that day. I was numb. The pain was palpable. My heart felt like it couldn't break any more.

Several days passed without any word from my doctor. I was dying to know what the results were of the fetal testing. Finally, the call came in from one of the nurses I had grown to love and trust in this process. "Hi, Bethanee. The results of your tests are in. First, I want to tell you how very sorry I am for your loss. There are no words I can express to convey how sad I am for you. Please know, we are here for you for whatever decisions you and Jason make. The results of the tests show there was nothing wrong with the baby. She was a perfectly healthy little girl."

To this day, I hear those exact words replay in my head. *"She was a perfectly healthy little girl."* That should've been good news. It *was* good news, but it was heartbreaking news at the same time. That meant she died for nothing. Nothing. My little girl would have been born fully capable of living outside of my womb. I didn't care if we had a child with disabilities, but that wasn't the reason she didn't survive. There were no answers. She was perfectly healthy.

I named her Hope. She was my *hope* that we could still, someday, have children.

In the following days, we received a huge outpouring of love from our friends and family. Over seventy-five cards were sent to our home with love, condolences, and prayers. Meals were made for our family; three bouquets of flowers were delivered to our home. That outpouring carried me through those dark and very lonely days. I still have all of those cards (and I don't keep anything!). I'm so thankful for those ladies who reached out to me and knew I needed strength and love.

Our doctors told us to wait at least two to three months before trying again. That was actually fine with me. I needed that time to heal. No amount of time would bring complete healing but waiting a few months would be helpful. So, we waited for three months. No one asked any questions. I liked it that way.

Three months passed and we met with the infertility doctor to discuss our next step. He suggested In-Vitro Fertilization (IVF). This would, hopefully, give us better chances for a sustainable pregnancy. We left there with leaflets of information, printed pages of information, and a lot of information in our heads. We left feeling completely unsure of the decision we would make. We had a lot of soul searching to do. Did we believe, ethically, in IVF? And if we did, what would we choose to do with any leftover embryos?

The ME: According to Dictionary.com, In-Vitro Fertilization (IVF) a specialized technique by which an ovum, especially a human one, is fertilized by sperm outside the body, with the resulting embryo later implanted in the uterus for gestation. In my own terms, it is a process by which the male sperm is washed and the female eggs are checked; then there is medical assistance in creating embryos outside the womb and medical diligence in growing them into strong, healthy embryos before transplanting them into the mother's womb.

After doing some research and discussing this option with one of my cousins, who had already walked down the IVF path, we decided we would do it. What we felt was right for us regarding IVF was to be sure to use up every single embryo, not allowing the doctors to discard any or use any for research (this is where IVF can get controversial). Whether they were created outside of my womb or naturally inside my womb, these embryos were all still God's creation and they were our babies, not a science project. We knew this meant the possibility of multiple attempts at IVF, and we also knew it could mean more children than we had been planning for, but we were more than happy to have as many children as God gave us. With that decision made, I called the doctor and informed him we would do IVF.

We had to finish waiting out the current month we were in. That was a long month. I had a new hope, though. God gave me a fresh outlook on getting pregnant, and possibly sustaining that pregnancy. Day 1 of the next month finally arrived. We labeled it "Day 1, Cycle 1." My hope and my prayer was that I would never have to look at a "Day 1, Cycle 10" or something awful like that. I had my ovulation stimulants and the progesterone (known as PIO—progesterone in oil) ready to go. I began "stimming" (medical slang for stimulating) that night. I took a deep sigh of relief when I injected the meds that night. I just knew (read hoped, begged, prayed!) this would be the answer.

The ME of IVF: When you first start IVF, at the beginning of a new month, you inject ovulation stimulants for roughly eleven to fourteen days, depending on how your body has responded to the stimulants in the past and depending on how long your cycle typically lasts. In those eleven to fourteen days I went to the infertility clinic for multiple blood tests and internal ultrasounds, all leading up to the "special IVF day." This process is very emotionally taxing and time-consuming. It's also very expensive if your insurance company doesn't cover it. Thankfully for us, ours covered most of these costs. But far too many insurance companies do not cover these costs, rendering IUIs and IVF obsolete. It's heartbreaking to know so many will not be able to reach their dreams of having a biological child, if that's their desire, simply because of a very broken system.

Now on day 10, I could tell I was very close to ovulation. I went to the clinic for my normal morning blood draw and ultrasound. Things had been looking really great! My cycle was progressing beautifully and everyone was excited with how my body was stimulating. I couldn't help but feel excited. During that morning's ultrasound, the nurse pointed out every single ovarian follicle. Each follicle on my ultrasound was growing just as they wanted to see. I had thirty-two follicles, otherwise known as *superovulation*. Yes, you're reading that right: thirty-two follicles in varying stages. Coming from IUI cycles, I knew that would be bad. But this was an IVF cycle, and I knew they

wanted multiple mature follicles. They needed multiple mature follicles and that's exactly what I had. The nurse didn't say much to me
that day except they wanted me to come back the next morning. Daily
visits were my norm at this point in a cycle.

The ME of Ovulation Stimulating: In the female reproductive
system, an ovarian follicle is a fluid-filled sac that contains an
immature egg, or *oocyte*. These follicles are found along the
lining of the ovaries. During ovulation, a mature egg is released
from a follicle. While several follicles begin to develop each
cycle, normally only one follicle will ovulate an egg at a time.
The follicles that do not release a mature egg disintegrate, and
this can happen at any stage of follicular development. Mature
follicles are the follicles that have an egg that's fully mature and
ready to be fertilized with sperm.[2]

I went in again the next day, which was Cycle Day 11. They drew
more blood and did another ultrasound. Again, thirty-two follicles.
This time the nurse pointed out all of the mature follicles. There were
nine! Nine beautifully, wonderfully mature eggs ready to go for my
first IVF cycle. I was so excited! The nurse seemed very pleased with
this too. As was normal, I drove home and waited for the next day's
instructions, which always came later in the day after they had time to
read blood test results and wait for the doctors to review everything. I
waited for the phone call to come and, in the meantime, called Jason
to inform him that the IVF procedure was likely going to happen on
Christmas Eve. He appreciated the heads up because he would have to

---

[2] www.verywell.com

take the day off of work if that was the case. We were both ready for whatever this IVF cycle would bring.

The call finally came, and I was in disbelief over the news. In preparation for the IVF procedure, they had called our insurance company to clear everything and realized something was wrong. Forms needed to be filled out, or some sort of special permission needed to be granted. I don't remember exactly what it was, all I remember is that the IVF procedure was canceled.

I tried my best to understand. I tried my hardest to figure out what was happening. I just couldn't emotionally process it all. At that moment, it seemed as if our walls of hope were collapsing on me. The hope I had felt for two months suddenly disappeared and faded into the abyss of yet another failed cycle. Only this time it wasn't the ovulation cycle that failed, it was the insurance process that failed. It was all about the money. We were faced with a decision: spend thousands of dollars out of pocket or do nothing. Those were the only two options we were given. It was heartbreaking. We had a little bit of money we had been saving for our eventual adoption—the one we both felt God leading us to do—but not for IVF. We didn't have thousands of dollars to drop for this process. It was a horrible situation to be in. We decided we would leave the money where it belonged and fully canceled the IVF cycle.

That night Jason and I lay in bed and talked. I cried for what felt like the millionth time and Jason held me, like he had become accustomed to doing. We discussed the events of the day and prayed together. Our doctors encouraged us not to have intercourse during the IVF cycle due to the risk of multiples. But that night we decided, *The heck with it . . . let's go for it.* This was hard for my play-by-the-rules personality, but Jason is a rule-breaker and didn't think twice about the risks. He thinks about the what-ifs and exciting possibilities.

The day after Christmas we left for winter vacation with my best friend and her family. We met them in Hershey, Pennsylvania—halfway between our home in New Hampshire and their home in Virginia. We expected to have some slightly good news for them, hoping that the cycle had gone well and that we would know in two weeks if we were expecting. Instead, we told them our IVF cycle had been canceled.

Sparing all the details, we tried to conceive multiple times on our own over that Christmas weekend and during vacation. For you curious readers, we had rented a small house where the kids were in a separate room and each couple had their own room. So the kids were well protected in their cozy beds in their cozy room. But we were going to do all we could do to the best of our ability to make something happen. The best-case scenario was that we would end up with twins or triplets—but we honestly didn't expect that. I was unable to get pregnant for three years without the help of IUIs and doctors. My broken body had failed me many times in the last three years, so what was the worst that could happen? With a new sense of hope, we "explored" the possibility of getting pregnant on our own.

A week later, after we were home from our trip to Pennsylvania, I began to *need* to know if our attempts were successful. The POAS (remember, *pee-on-a-stick*) craze came back with a vengeance. Strange, I know, but I tried to POAS *every single time* I went to the bathroom, hoping and praying for that double line—the sign of life growing inside of me.

The day before I was supposed to get my period, marking the end of this opportunity, I saw it—there was a faint line on the pregnancy test. I did my ritualistic dance of running to every window with natural light and holding it under every house light option. No matter where I held the stick, I could see that faint line. Fear, excitement, nervousness, and joy overtook me. I was a mixed bag of emotions, but we were pregnant on our own (well, kind of)! I held this information quiet for the rest of the day. I wanted to scream it out loud, but I didn't. I wanted to see what the "magic sticks" would read tomorrow before I would say something. Would there be lines or no lines? The next day came and the very first thing I did was POAS—again. There they were: those two lines. It was real. I was pregnant. We were pregnant.

I needed to call my doctor. I knew I needed to come clean about breaking the rules, but I was afraid to tell him what we had done. The rule-follower in me wanted Jason to make that call, but I called anyway. I told the doctor that I was getting a positive pregnancy test and asked if I could come in for a blood test. They were happy to do that for me, so I went in and did the test then waited at home for the news, again. The doctor's office called later that day and confirmed I was, indeed, pregnant. I still hadn't seen the doctor, but I was dreading that face-to-face so I was okay with waiting another day. After confirming the pregnancy, they scheduled a five-week ultrasound. I suspect it was to determine how many babies I was carrying so they could give me the options for "selective reduction" if there were more than two. But there was no way *that* was going to happen at any point, with any number. Every life conceived is a life given by God and that was not a life we were about to take because the doctors didn't like our odds. That would never have been an option for us.

Jason and I went in for my five-week ultrasound. I still remember the nervous excitement. We knew we were expecting and we were hoping there would at least be twins so we could say we were "done."

We were not the kind of people who desperately wanted twins, but at this point, with all of our infertility issues and recurrent miscarriages, we were more than happy to have multiple babies and be done with the whole IVF process.

The doctor came into the ultrasound room—something he never did during those early ultrasounds. I smiled nervously, waiting to get chewed out by him. He was polite, professional, and kind. He congratulated us then went into a very brief "the-potential-for-mul-tiples-is-high-and-the-risks-would-be-even-higher-if-you-are . . ." lecture. We understood and acknowledged his caution but informed him that we were willing to take that risk. He was okay with our answer and we quickly moved onto the ultrasound. Within minutes, he located a baby. He thoroughly scanned for signs of another baby, but he could not find one. There we were, with one five-week-old baby growing inside of me. I was flooded with a range of emotions—relief that there were not nine babies, joy and thankfulness for the baby we saw on the monitor, and a deep sadness at the realization of how broken my body really was. I was both sad and overjoyed that nine mature eggs produced one baby.

All throughout my infertility journey, I was part of an online support group for women struggling with infertility. We had become a close-knit online family, generally free of judgment and the typical online lashings you find elsewhere. My online friends wanted to know what the results were that day so, once I got home, I posted the results from the ultrasound. Up until that point, I felt safe in that group so I also shared the range of emotions that accompanied my ultrasound report. What I was not prepared for, however, were the lashings that would come from this community—my "support" group, because they misinterpreted my sadness about there being one baby as something to not be thankful for, but in reality, it was a realization of how broken my body really was. That is why I was sad and that was what they couldn't understand. I realized that day that I had built a false sense of security based on limited interactions with these women whom I had never met. My truth saddened me. No matter how many times you go through infertility, miscarriage, and pregnancy, it's sad to realize your body does not function the way you know it's supposed to. It's sad to realize your body is failing you and your body is the reason for all the heartache and trials you and your spouse are facing. We were more than thrilled with the new little bean growing inside of me. And we were more than happy with the simplicity only one baby brings. I was just sad for my body. It took me a long time (I'm talking *years*) to process those emotions. And, honestly, I still carry those emotions and memories of infertility and miscarriage with me.

****

Helpful Hint: If this is YOU, going through infertility and recurrent miscarriages:

Ladies, even if you're in a support group, as I was, we must realize that we are all different. Every story is different and every person is different. We all process life in different ways, depending on our family of origin, our personalities, our life experiences, our marriages, and so much more. At the time, I felt I owed each of those women an explanation because I hated the thought of being misunderstood.

Older and wiser now, I realize I did not owe anything to anyone. I had a right to my own emotions. There is no one who should be telling you how to feel on this incredibly tumultuous roller coaster ride, even women who have walked a similar road. We are all doing the best we can. And we must remember this about ourselves and about others. Your emotions do not need to be validated by others, nor swept under the rug. Cry on, sweet sisters. It's hard, it stinks, and it's painful! But you will survive.

****

After coming to grips with how my body was failing, I was able to rejoice more sweetly in the one little bean that was growing in me. This baby was clearly an answer to prayer and a miracle from God. Now we just prayed fervently for this pregnancy to survive to full-term.

The ultrasounds and blood tests were frequent. I visited the doctor's office often and injected the progesterone (PIO) shots into my hip nightly. At my thirteen-week appointment, the doctor told me I could stop the PIO shots because my body had started producing enough progesterone to support the pregnancy now that I was in my second trimester. I had entered my second trimester successfully! Sweet bliss. I breathed a huge sigh of relief. I had never miscarried in the second trimester so we were feeling positive and began accepting the idea that this little bean might just make it into our arms. We finally shared the news with everyone, and we let ourselves feel the excitement too.

The pregnancy progressed very smoothly. We began discussing possible names. We found a name with a perfect meaning, and the name happened to be gender-neutral. We decided on Jaidyn if it was a girl or Jaden if it was a boy. The name means "God has heard." If the baby was a girl, the middle name would be Noelle. We chose this middle name because the full meaning of her name, Jaidyn Noelle, would be

"God has heard—Christmas." If we put Jaidyn Noelle into a sentence, it meant "God has heard (our prayers) (on) Christmas." We loved it! It was so perfect considering all we had gone through. We waited out the remainder of the pregnancy to find out the baby's gender. The day for my scheduled cesarean came and my doctor announced to us we had a new baby girl! Our little miracle baby, Jaidyn Noelle, was born on September 1, 2005, all 6 pounds 15 ounces of her. God had indeed heard our prayers on Christmas morning, nine months prior to her birth.

CHAPTER 6

SEPARATED

We were blessed and we knew that. We were so very in love with our three little miracles and we knew what a gift they were. At five, Caleb was fully on track with all his motor and verbal skills and you'd never have known there'd ever been any concerns with him. Tiera, four, was growing and her little personality was shining through. Little Jaidyn was a few months old and changing daily.

Life was beautiful.

With all that had happened trying to bring little Jaidyn into our lives, we decided we would not wait to conceive another baby. If we ended up with two children close in age again we were okay with that, but we didn't want to take the chance of going through another three and a half years of waiting. So, with that, we went straight to our fertility specialist when Jaidyn was just three months old. We told him we were ready to begin the process again, and thus began the trials of conceiving baby number four.

It didn't take long to get back on the IUI train. We easily slid back into the routine of blood work, ultrasounds, and doctor appointments.

Month after month passed by with no results. Then a year passed. So much frustration and confusion. So many unanswered questions. The whole thing was maddening. Our insurance still did not cover IVF and we made the commitment to *not* dip into our adoption fund for an IVF cycle, so we were stuck with the IUI cycle—hoping, dreaming, and praying.

Finally, we got the good news we had been waiting for. I tested positive with an at-home test *and* the doctor's blood test. Considering our history, this was only mildly good news. We knew not to get too excited, so we just waited for a bit to see if the pregnancy was going to stick. A few close friends and family members knew our news and they began praying for us. Our little bean made it to six weeks when I began miscarrying. I remember I was on the phone with my mom when I felt the gush. I started gasping and saying, "I think I just started miscarrying, Mom." My mom was in shock and I was in disbelief. Just like that, it was over. One year of trying, and it was all over within two weeks. I cried and allowed myself to feel sad, but I didn't let it rock my world. Maybe I was just numb from all of my miscarriages, or maybe my fear of miscarrying protected me from getting too attached to the pregnancy. But I have to say, I was thankful to not be feeling completely broken and beaten down this time.

We picked up the pieces of another shattered dream and began again with the very next cycle. Sigh. We all wanted the train ride or train wreck (depending on the day) to end, but we just knew we were supposed to press on. Again, people questioned us. They questioned why we didn't just give up and live "contently" with what God had given us.

****

Helpful Hint: If this is YOU, being questioned about your decisions to keep pressing on:

All I can say is, when you're in the situation, you will know. Or when you're trying to build a family and your dreams, hopes, and visions for your family don't come to pass, you will know the pain, heartache, longing, and desires to do so, even through tough situations. What I can say is that I'm very thankful Jesus didn't give up on us when things got tough. He pressed in and He pressed onward with us. You need to do what you sense God is leading you and your spouse to do. Don't let the world's expectations drown out the dreams and hopes you've prayed about and are believing for. For Jason and me, that was another child.

****

Onward we went.

Three or four months passed by with no pregnancy. I was near the middle of a cycle when my POAS (pee-on-a-stick) impulse went into overdrive again. The day before I was due to get my blood drawn at the lab, I took a home test and saw a very faint line. It gave me enough hope to cling to that day. At this point, I was also giving myself the progesterone injections, so I had to remember that the progesterone could lead to false positives. I went in for my morning blood draw and waited for the results to come in later that day. The results were positive! Wow. Only four months after our last miscarriage and we were pregnant again. That alone was a miracle. This news brought us back to the very familiar place of praying and hoping for this little bean to survive.

I went in for blood work every forty-eight hours to confirm that my human chorionic gonadotropin (HCG) numbers were doubling as they should've been, and they were! HCG is a hormone that increases once an embryo (fertilized egg) implants into the lining of the uterus. We decided not to keep this one a secret because we wanted people praying. And we had so many people praying for us!

Things were looking great and progressing well with the pregnancy. My HCG numbers continued to double and increase accordingly. We were beginning to get excited. I was already ten weeks pregnant. I gave regular updates at my moms groups, prayer groups, and to our pastor's wife, Sam. She and I were very good friends. She had asked me to call her after my ten-week appointment, but I didn't get a chance. I saw our little bean and everything looked great. On the ultrasound monitor the baby's measurements were all great, including the heart rate. Things were stable and there was nothing to worry about. Two more weeks and I would be out of the first trimester.

The day after my ten-week checkup, I was out running errands when I remembered I hadn't called Sam. So when I stopped at the gas station to gas up my car, I decided to call her just to let her know that everything was great. She answered the phone right away. With excitement in my voice, I started telling her about the baby and all the good news from the day before . . . when I felt the gush. Another breathtaking and mind-numbing moment. I was miscarrying again.

I stopped mid-sentence with Sam and said, "I think I'm miscarrying right now. Like, right this very moment." I'll never forget what it felt like to experience such a sharp shift in my mood within a blink of an eye. One moment I was telling her my good news about the baby and how well the pregnancy was going. The next moment I was telling her that I was miscarrying. By this point I knew what was "normal" and what wasn't. For all three of my full-term pregnancies, I never even spotted, let alone gushed. I began to cry and she began to pray for me. To this day, I am so very grateful for Sam—for her steadfast friendship in all of those trying times. She was so constant. She was the one who watched our children while we were going through some of the infertility procedures and was with me emotionally during the miscarriages and the emotional roller coaster of loss and life. Her friendship was such a gift sent from God.

The moment we got off the phone, I called Jason and my doctor to inform them both. Jason was mostly silent. He hadn't believed the pregnancy was going to stick from the very beginning. He wanted to, but it was his way of protecting himself, and I couldn't blame him. There was too much history of loss already.

My doctor wanted me to come in for another D&C procedure. But I decided to deliver my baby on my own this time. I gave my body time to miscarry, as it was designed and created to do, because this time I knew better. And when we know better, we do better. That meant allowing my body to do what it was already naturally doing. I know there may be times when a D&C is necessary, but this was not the time. The doctor's office told me to bring in a sample of the baby if I wanted testing done again. If I had delivered a whole baby, I wouldn't have considered bringing in a sample of tissue. But there was nothing in my miscarriage discharge that even remotely resembled a baby, so I decided I would bring in some of the tissue I had. The results of the tissue testing told us the baby was a perfectly healthy little girl. I named her Aliyah, which means "to ascend." She had ascended into heaven ahead of us.

I was crushed and broken, again. Tears flooded my eyes for days.

After this particular loss, I clearly remember my husband telling me we should go to church, if for no other reason than to be in the presence of God and surrounded by close friends. I didn't want to, though. I wanted to stay hidden in my pain in my house. I didn't want to have to look at anyone or see anyone trying to avoid me because they hurt for me and they didn't know what to say or do. But Jason insisted, so we packed up the kids and went to church. I made it through one worship song and half of another, but I couldn't do it any longer. I couldn't keep the fake smile painted on my face. I ran to the bathroom where I collapsed on the floor and just began to weep. All I wanted to do was go home, be alone, and cry.

I started to lose my sense of self in the wake of this heartache, loss, and pain. It was incredibly isolating and lonely. I wish I could say I had the perfect answer for what to do about the way I was feeling—the way so many of us feel when we experience multiple miscarriages—but I didn't. And I still don't have the answers. I never joined a local, face-to-face support group. Maybe that would've helped. I was seriously wondering if all of this heartache was worth it. Jason and I would have to have some serious conversations if we were going to continue this process.

But what I did know for certain is that there was—and still is—a God who cared deeply for me in those painful moments. So, I clung to Him. Clinging to God didn't take away my loneliness, but it did give me an outlet; it gave me a safe place to cry and scream, a safe place to let my emotions go so when I was out in public and with friends I didn't have to feel so alone. The hardest moments were those immediately after each of the miscarriages, those moments when news had gotten out that I was pregnant and lost another baby. I felt deeply isolated. People either avoided making eye contact with me or avoided me altogether.

Still, I never once felt God was doing this *to* me. Having all of these miscarriages was simply a result of my broken body. God had already been so faithful to give me three of the best gifts here on earth—Caleb, Tiera, and Jaidyn.

> *I lift up my eyes to the mountains—*
> *where does my help come from?*
> *My help comes from the LORD,*
> *the Maker of heaven and earth.*
>
> Psalm 121:1–2 NIV

Two months after our *seventh* miscarriage, we were thrown a curveball. Out of the blue, Jason was offered a job in Washington, DC. If we moved there, we would lose our doctors and the fertility clinic we had become so familiar with. We would have to start all over—developing a new infertility treatment protocol. And the new clinic would want to run additional tests. I was overwhelmed at the thought, but maybe it was just the change we needed.

After a couple of months of praying about the position, we decided Jason would take the job. We both sensed God had opened that door, even though there were still some unclear details. So, we packed up enough clothing for a few weeks, including some toys for the three kids. We loaded the car with our belongings, including the cat and the fish, and said our goodbyes to our dear friends in New Hampshire and family in Maine. We decided on temporary housing in Virginia to give us time to sell our house in New Hampshire. As soon as we were settled, I began looking for a new clinic. It had already been a year and a half since beautiful Jaidyn had been born, and I didn't want to waste any more time on trying to conceive. I found the infertility support groups I needed in the local DC area and started getting recommendations for infertility clinics.

As I was collecting data on various clinics, my friend Sam called to tell me about a young nineteen-year-old girl who had just started going to our old church back in NH. This young woman—we will call her Melissa—was a few weeks pregnant with twins. Twins! Melissa had decided she could not raise the babies on her own and confided in our pastor's wife that she was thinking about putting the babies up for adoption. Sam thought of us right away. She knew we were struggling to get pregnant again and she also knew of our desire to adopt someday. Sam asked if she could share our contact information with the girl.

When Jason got home that night I sat him down to tell him about the phone call. Adoption was absolutely in our plan because we sensed God had put it on our hearts before we were married. Even though we were going through more infertility struggles, we had not actively looked into adoption yet. However, we thought maybe God was bringing adoption to us. We decided to prayerfully engage in conversations with this young woman. We began talking on the phone with Melissa and she began opening up to us about her situation, her home life, and the pregnancy.

We had been living in DC for about three months when Jason and I started to realize we were in a sticky situation. Our house in New Hampshire was not selling and the temporary housing we were in was just that: *temporary*. We had been given three months in the temporary housing with Jason's government contract, and our time was up. With a house payment in New Hampshire, we simply could not afford to continue paying rent in DC at four thousand dollars a month (his company was paying for that). Frankly, we couldn't afford *any* place in DC with a house on the market in New Hampshire. This left us in quite the conundrum. Jason was stuck in DC with a two-year appointment at a government agency, and the kids and I had to go back to New Hampshire.

Jason helped us load the car, prayed with us, and kissed us all goodbye. Caleb, Tiera, Jaidyn, and I made the long drive back to New Hampshire without him. We agreed that our new family routine would be Jason working in DC Monday through Thursday, then flying home every Thursday night after work to spend a three-day weekend with us. We were all sad, but we grew so much as a family in those two years. We made our marriage and our family a huge priority. The hardest decision we made in that season was sending out an email to all of our friends to say that we loved them but would be unable to spend any weekends with them (except for special occasions like weddings, birthdays, graduations, etc.) because we needed to make our family a priority in this capacity.

Once the kids and I were resettled in our house in New Hampshire, we immediately began to attend our old church again. The first Sunday we were back, we met Melissa. She was a lovely girl with dark, curly hair, big brown eyes, and a nice smile. It was hard to see her little baby bump growing because of her stocky build, but eventually she asked the church for some maternity clothes. Our church rallied around her and around us. Jason and I pulled together some money so she could buy some clothes. The kids and I began building a relationship with her. We talked on the phone frequently and she would update me on the pregnancy, movements of the babies, and so on. It was all feeling so real as the weeks and months passed. How could our adoption story be so easy? But we were more than okay with that because we had already gone through our fair share of heartache while trying to conceive another child. We welcomed the ease with which this was all happening.

By Mother's Day 2007, Melissa's pregnancy was somewhere late in the second trimester or early in the third. Jason was home that weekend, and Caleb and Tiera had prepared me a lovely breakfast of Cheerios, room-temperature milk, a spilled glass of orange juice, and an adorably written note wishing me a Happy Mother's Day. The phone rang around 9:00 a.m. The kids were upstairs playing, and Jason was still sound asleep in bed. I picked up the phone, heard Melissa's voice, and settled on the couch for one of our routine conversations. This time she sounded troubled. I could tell something was wrong. I asked her if she was okay, and she started to cry. She told me she had delivered the babies that day and didn't know how to tell us.

She said the babies were small—three and a half pounds each. I was pleasantly surprised by their weight, thinking this was bigger than I anticipated at this point. But they were having medical problems—problems breathing, problems with their heart, eyes, and lungs. She worried if we would still want to adopt the babies as they would most likely have lifelong disabilities. She wasn't sure the babies were even going to make it through the next twenty-four hours. She asked me if we still wanted the babies, and I responded with a firm "YES!" I continued, "We told you we would adopt your babies . . . not on the condition of them being healthy only. We would adopt them no matter what happens."

My mind was racing and my heart was sinking. I asked her if I could call our pastor and his wife, Sam, to tell them what was happening so we could get some people praying for her and the babies. She said she didn't want anyone to know that she had given birth to the babies.

Hmmm.

I asked if I could come see her and meet the babies. She said she didn't want anyone at the hospital yet.

Hmmm.

I asked her what hospital she was at so I could send some flowers to her and she said, "I don't want anyone to know where I am right now."

Between her answers and the weights she had given me for the babies (remember, three and a half pounds *each*), red flags were flying and I knew something was wrong. I politely got off the phone with her and immediately called Sam. I began asking her questions about this young girl.

"Do you know where her parents live? Have you ever met them? Do you know her back-story?"

And so on.

I needed answers. I got a little more information on Melissa and began doing some investigative work.

First, I started with the hospitals in our area. I began systematically calling all the hospitals nearest us. Then I moved to hospitals that were farther away but still in the same state (we live within one hour of the New Hampshire, Massachusetts, Maine, and Vermont borders). It turns out that hospitals don't appreciate random strangers calling to find out if twins have been born at their hospital. I got yelled at several times, and a few other times I was politely informed of "standard hospital safety protocol." After giving my story with each call, I was able to get just enough information from each hospital to allow me to move on. Even if it was a blanket statement—"No twins have been born here in the last week or two"—that was enough for me.

I began questioning everything and thinking back over my conversations with Melissa. *Was every word out of her mouth a lie? Were*

there ever twins? Was she pregnant at all? Or was she simply chang-
ing her mind and made up this whole story to get out of putting them
up for adoption? Either way, I was not going down without a fight. I
wanted answers, and I was going to find them if it killed me.

At this point in my investigative work I knew Melissa's parents
lived in the small town next to ours, so I decided to look up their last
name in the white pages. I started to call every single person in that
town with that last name. Thank goodness we did not live in New York
City or Los Angeles! Their town had around seven thousand residents,
so I knew there wouldn't be too many people with the same last name.
I began calling each person listed in the white pages with her last
name. It took only three calls. On the third call a man answered the
phone. I introduced myself.

"Hello, my name in Bethanee. Do you know someone by the name
of Melissa ?"

"Yes, I have a sister by that name. Is everything okay?"

I described Melissa to him and he said, "Yes, that's definitely my
sister. What's going on?"

"I just need to know if she had her babies this morning."

"Babies? What babies?"

I shared our story, sparing no details. And, as if it happened yesterday, I can still hear his response hanging in the air like a bomb had
gone off:

"Oh my God, I'm so sorry. You're the fourth couple she has done
this to. I'm so sorry for the pain she has caused you. She is nineteen
and we've been trying to get her into a mental hospital but we can't
force her to because she's not a minor. I'm so sorry for your loss. I'm
sorry for what she has done to you and your family."

I felt numb. How could someone be so cruel? How could someone care so little for people's feelings and do something so intentional and over such a long period of time? It was incredibly painful. Then the realization sank in that she had not only done something cruel, but she had done it on Mother's Day. That Mother's Day was unbearably hard. I sat on the couch, my muscles shaking from adrenaline, my face soaked with tears, and my heart broken, once again. I had to get up and tell my family now. How do you tell your family—your sweet, innocent children—about the cruelty of human beings? It grieved me that I had to do it.

Even though I was broken, and even though Jason and I were shaken, we used that moment to bring it all back to the cross of Jesus. I needed our children to remember that even when evil prevails, the goodness of Jesus ultimately wins! I needed our children to know that Jesus Christ has already paid the price for the sins Melissa had committed against us, and that we needed to remember to pray for those who hurt us. It wasn't what I wanted to do, but it's what we *needed* to do. So, after we gathered the kids to tell them this heartbreaking news on Mother's Day afternoon, we ended our conversation by reading a family devotional and praying for Melissa. We prayed that our own hearts would heal and that our broken hearts would be filled with peace. We also prayed for the Holy Spirit to fill Melissa's heart. We knew that more than anything else, she needed to know the Savior, Jesus Christ.

Back home in New Hampshire, with no adoption happening, we had a decision to make. We discussed our options: end our attempts to conceive another baby and officially begin the adoption process, or find a new doctor that could help us with infertility treatments. With Jason's new job in DC, most infertility treatments were not covered so we had to find a doctor who was covered under our new insurance. Everything would be out of pocket for us this time, which meant we had a very narrow chance of conceiving another baby. In fact, we weren't even sure of the actual cost of a full IUI cycle yet so we didn't know how many times we would be able to try.

After praying about what to do, Jason and I decided we would try to conceive baby number four. Between our own hearts and the vision God had given us for our family, we just did not seem finished with the three.

Helpful Hint: If you've been here before or think you will be here someday, or you know someone going through this painful journey:

This is where I would say, again, to anyone reading this: *You do not know the plans God has given to anyone or what He has put in their hearts. You should not presume to know what's best for anyone. This is not the time to tell a sweet family looking to expand, "Why can't you just be content with the three you have?" or "Why don't you stop putting yourself through this? It's your choice." Those comments are harmful—and we heard them more frequently than I'd like to admit. These comments are harmful to your relationship with that person and hurtful to the couple going through infertility.*

So to those who have made harmful comments like this, hear me when I say this: The couple would not be going through this process if they didn't want more babies. They would not be going through all of this if it weren't important to them. So, support them. That doesn't mean you have to agree with them, but it does mean that you need to keep your thoughts to yourself and simply pray for them. Hug them. Support them with encouraging emails, texts, messages, and hugs, and show your greatest support by not saying hurtful things.

****

It didn't take me long to find a new specialist. During our first visit, he listened to my whole story of infertility and recurrent miscarriages, and then he told me some really great news. His office took back all sealed and unused medicine from patients who become pregnant and no longer needed it. Even better, they donated the unopened stimulants to families who were struggling with infertility but didn't have insurance coverage or the funds to pay for medication. This was such a blessing and a true gift from God! What we thought was going to be a big expense was now covered by free meds! We just needed to pay for ultrasounds, blood work, and the IUI itself. What an answer to prayer.

So, we began at the start of my next cycle. When Cycle Day 1 came around I waited for my instructions. I started giving myself the same daily injections I had in years past. This round was very different, though. Jason was still living in DC Monday through Thursday, so I had to bring the kids with me to all of those early morning drives and two-minute doctor visits.

Our routine went something like this: every Monday morning I would wake all the kids up at four, load them into the car with their blankies, stuffed animals, and coats. Then we would drive Jason to the airport. If I had a blood draw that morning, I would proceed to the doctor's office where I would sit in the parking lot and wait for the office to open at six while the kids slept in the car. Then I'd wake up the kids, head into the lab for blood work, and go home. If I didn't have to go in on the mornings when we dropped Jason off, then I'd get home around five, walk the kids back to their beds, and we'd all sleep for a few more hours. On the days we didn't have to do an airport run, I'd wake the kids up around 5:30 a.m., load them into the car with all their bedtime belongings, drive myself to the doctor's, get all the kids out of the car, go into the doctor's office for a two-minute blood draw and the occasional ultrasound, then pack them back up, drive home, and put them all back into bed. It was awful! I look back now and wonder how on earth I managed to do this routine without any help.

Things were progressing well. But there was a new problem—I needed Jason at home. I needed him there for "the special visit" required at a certain point in our IUI cycle. We discussed freezing Jason's sperm so it wouldn't matter if he was in the state or not on any given day, but it actually looked like he might make it home in time, at least for this one cycle. We all kept a close eye on the calendar. Our doctor thought he might even be able to push my meds to a higher dosage so I could give myself the HCG (ovulation stimulant) shot a day or two earlier than he originally thought was optimal. So, we went with this plan. Normally we would do the HCG shots around Cycle Day 13 for me. But this time we would be doing it on Cycle Day 11. Our doctor was confident we would still be in a good spot.

Cycle Day 11 arrived. We just barely made it in time for the procedure before Jason had to fly to DC at 5:30 the next morning. It was a Sunday morning and we had to be at the office at eight. We also had church that morning so we put a good "spit-shine" on the kids, got ourselves ready for church, then left for the appointment. The appointment went well overall. Sparing the details, there were a few minor hiccups. But nothing big, so we were back on the road in time to get to church.

The next morning at four, we woke the kids up, strapped them into the car, and drove Jason to the airport. We were hopeful. This cycle was in God's hands either way, but I was so hopeful it would work out because I felt like it just *had* to work out this time due to all of the hard work I put into the last two weeks. Waking up the kids in the wee morning hours and driving to the doctor's office all by myself was *hard*. The stress of trying to time a cycle, which cannot be easily timed by doctors and not at all by me, was also hard. However, I was realistic enough to know this was our first attempt in several months, and we just did not get pregnant that easily. I reminded myself that it had taken an entire year of unsuccessful attempts to get pregnant prior to moving to DC. But, I hoped and I prayed.

In the meantime, Jason and I kept up our routine. As my cycle progressed I began to get anxious. I was giving myself the progesterone injections daily, hoping they would sustain a pregnancy if I was actually pregnant. I began to POAS around Cycle Day 19, a full nine days prior to my blood test and a scheduled period. Nothing was showing up, not even a faint line. The day came for my scheduled blood work to determine if I was pregnant or not. I went in for the blood work with the kids, then took them home where we all fell back to sleep. After waking up, I waited for the phone call. The call finally came midafternoon:

"Bethanee, we want to let you know the results of your test this morning. We are happy to inform you that you are expecting!"

The nurse went on to say, "We know your history, so we want to keep a very close eye on you and the baby. We are going to increase the amount of progesterone you're using and we don't want you to do anything active, at all. And we want you to abstain from intercourse until you are out of your first trimester."

I was in shock.

After *seven* miscarriages I knew not to get too excited about the news. But there was still a little life growing inside of me. All of those pregnancies were babies worthy of my love, excitement, and joy. I just knew I had to temper my excitement with the reality of so many losses and the very real chance this little one might not see life outside of my broken womb. But here we were—pregnant again—and I was shocked that it happened on our first IUI attempt since being back in New Hampshire.

Because our insurance was different this time around, all of the early pregnancy blood work and ultrasounds were not an option. I had to walk through the first few weeks of my pregnancy mostly blind. I comforted myself with the reminder that it wasn't as if the early ultrasounds ever protected me from miscarrying. If anything, the early ultrasounds gave me a false sense of security. This time I had one early ultrasound at six weeks, and that was it.

Everything I did, I did cautiously. I didn't lift anything heavy, didn't run, didn't work out, didn't have intercourse. I did next to nothing. The kids did what they could and Jason helped out as much as possible (and the house got messy!). I was super cautious. We finally made it past the first trimester. *Was this it? Did this mean that baby number four would actually be born?*

That winter was brutal. New Hampshire saw record amounts of snow (105 inches to be exact!) and it seemed like there was a major snow storm every Monday morning and Thursday evening when Jason was flying to and from DC. This meant I had to shovel snow all winter . . . a lot of snow. With Jason gone and no teenagers at home, the shoveling was up to me. I'm the first to admit that I was *really* afraid to shovel because I didn't want to do anything that might contribute to another miscarriage. But we didn't have a garage to cover our car, so I really didn't have a choice. I had to shovel! When the first big snow arrived, my sweet eight-year-old Caleb (who was no longer paralyzed on his left side and was, in fact, left-handed!) met me outside all dressed up in his snow gear and told me, "Mom, I've got this. You go inside so you don't miscarry. I want my baby brother or sister to live."

I cried. I was so proud of him! He had such a thoughtful, tender heart and he loved this little one growing inside of me just as much as I did. He had witnessed me in so much pain throughout the years and he wanted to spare me more. I watched out the window many times that winter as that little "big" boy shoveled snow, storm after storm. It both melted and broke my heart.

I successfully entered the second trimester and all was going great with my pregnancy! We had our twenty-week ultrasound and found out we were having a little girl, much to the chagrin of our son, who desperately wanted a baby brother. We were thrilled to see she appeared to be healthy and developing well. We could finally begin to really celebrate this pregnancy. Major milestones had been reached and crossed. We eventually set a date for the cesarean.

On July 11, 2008, Ivory Grace was born into our family, and she forever changed my life. In the minutes after her birth, the doctors confirmed what Jason and I already knew: we were done having babies! They wanted to confirm this decision by tying my tubes. We gave them an undeniable yes! Not because we were done adding to our family but because we were done with everything it took to get us four healthy biological children. Moments later, the surgeon told me they had begun the procedure to tie my tubes. Jason and I held Ivory together between the two of us as I lay on the operating table and cried tears of joy and relief.

It was all a bit surreal.

For ten years we had been doing everything possible to get

pregnant, and now we were on the complete opposite side of the spectrum. Having my tubes tied seemed unnecessary given our difficulties getting pregnant, but we also didn't want to face an unplanned pregnancy and more miscarriages. We would've gladly taken on more pregnancies, but the real reason for having my tubes tied was all the miscarriages, the injections, the uncertainty, and the heartbreak. I just couldn't do it anymore.

I started to cry. The nurses and anesthesiologist all cooed and awed over our beautiful little Ivory. They all thought she was the reason I was crying. In part, they were right. She *was* beautiful and I *was* feeling an enormous amount of joy, pride, and thankfulness for the gift that had just been given to me. But I was also crying because the sheer weight of the last ten years was *finally* lifting off my shoulders.

In those moments I knew there would never be another heart-wrenching miscarriage or injection into my abdomen or hip or 6:00 a.m. doctor's appointment for blood work or ultrasound. I was overwhelmed with emotion. I finally felt like I could breathe. All of the pressure was gone—the pressure of tracking my cycle so closely, wondering if I was pregnant, or worse, the fear and anxiety of the first trimester. It was all gone. Our biological children were here, and they were healthy, handsome, and beautiful. They were truly the joy of our lives. Our hearts were full beyond measure.

CHAPTER 7

TEN YEARS LATER

As I write this chapter the date is October 15. It's ironic that I'm wrapping up our story of our infertility and loss today because it is National Pregnancy and Infant Loss Awareness Day. Now almost ten years later, I write about those seven little lives we lost because they are still my children. I speak about them because they had no voice to do so on their own. I don't want them to be forgotten because they are not forgotten by me. Their loss created a huge hole in my heart. And I know I'm not alone. Statistics show that one in four women will experience a miscarriage. That's a lot of loss.

Those years of infertility and miscarriages were some of the darkest years of my life. The loss felt unbearable at times. However, I'm so very

*You were here for a moment . . .
but left a lifetime of love.*

March of Dimes

grateful for what I learned about myself in those years. I learned that *I am a survivor. I am dedicated. I am consistent. I am driven. And I am a fighter.* And I am thankful that God was with me all along the way helping me through all of the loss, and in the process, helping me learn how to handle difficult situations.

If you are reading this book and you are not a person of faith, I want to encourage you with this: *There is a great strength that comes from knowing God. He is the only Comforter who can provide you with the peace you need in hard times.*

If you are a person of faith, then I want to encourage you with this: *Please think before you speak.* The Christian community around us often tried to comfort me with misquoted Scripture. I remember someone once saying, "Bethanee, don't worry! God won't give you more than you can handle." That response always felt like a slap in the face because I often felt like *all* of it was more than I could handle. I finally looked up that Bible verse because I wanted to understand the full context. I was so thankful I did because knowing the context of this verse alleviated the frustration and hurt I received from its misquotation. The actual passage from 1 Corinthians 10:13 (NIRV) says:

> *You are tempted in the same way all other human beings are. God is faithful. He will not let you be tempted any more than you can take. But when you are tempted, God will give you a way out. Then you will be able to deal with it.*

There was a stark difference between those two messages: *God won't give you more than you can handle* and *God won't let you be tempted any more than you can take.* This was important for me to realize because most days my journey was more than I could handle. Knowing the truth gave me more freedom to feel what I was feeling: overwhelmed and crushed from the sheer weight of our loss. And then

I thought about Christians in other countries who were being tortured and imprisoned for their faith. I thought about women and children caught in the sex slave trade, being raped and abused every day. I thought about families who had lost loved ones to fire, accidents, murder, natural disasters, disease, and more. All of that is *way more* than we can handle, except we have the grace of God with us. Life happens. Bad things happen to good people because we live in a broken, fallen world. And my broken body was no different. But God was always with me, always covering me with His grace and His love. There were times in my darkest moments when I may have doubted God, asking, "Why me? Why again?" But I knew that He actually never left my side.

Sometimes God's presence during my darkest days looked like notes of condolence and letters of love in the mail. Sometimes it was a long hug from a friend. Sometimes it was a meal made by someone in our community. Sometimes it was a poem, a sermon, or meme that spoke words of love, encouragement, and hope to our hurting hearts. So often these words encouraged me about the future God had set before us.

In those moments, I drew strength from these words spoken by Moses to Joshua in Deuteronomy 31:6 (NLT):

So be strong and courageous! Do not be afraid and do not panic before them. For the Lord your God will personally go ahead of you. He will neither fail you nor abandon you.

Just two verses down we see God remind us *again* that He will not leave us and, in fact, He goes ahead of us, preparing a way and a path. Deuteronomy 31:8 (NLT) tells us,

Do not be afraid or discouraged, for the Lord will personally go ahead of you. He will be with you; he will neither fail you nor abandon you.

God had been preparing a way for us all along—throughout our journey of infertility, our miscarriages, and our adoption story. And He's been preparing a way for you too.

Helpful Hint if you are a friend or family member of someone who has had a miscarriage:

I would like to encourage those of you reading this book to remember to be there for your daughter, sister, or friend if she's facing a miscarriage or pregnancy loss. Don't speak unless you're willing to speak words of love and comfort to her. And remember, what you think may be words of encouragement and comfort may actually be words that unintentionally hurt her. So, if you want to speak words of encouragement, say something like, "I'm so sorry this is happening to you," or "What can I do to help you?" or "How can I pray for you?" or "I want you to know I'm here for you." Keep your counsel to yourself. Offer your hand so she can hold it, offer your shoulder for her to cry on, and offer your help with daily chores like laundry and meals. However, please keep your advice and your opinions to yourself. This is not the time for that in her life. She is broken and hurting.

****

PART TWO

OUR ADOPTION JOURNEY

CHAPTER 8

FIRST STOP: HAITI

As we began the adoption process I started a blog to keep family and friends updated on our process. The general consensus was to expect a two-year journey, whether the adoption was international, domestic, private, or through the foster care system. Because we had already walked a long, hard road with infertility, my heart wished the adoption process would go so much faster. But in my head, I knew we could be in for a long journey. And what I was completely and utterly *not* prepared for was the mental anguish of adoption.

Jason and I had planned to adopt since we first met at the ages of nineteen and twenty years. We had been saving for adoption for a long time—praying about it, talking about it, and doing our research long before we ever started the process. But there is nothing that could have prepared us for what we went through, which may sound odd considering we had already experienced loss in regards to adoption (remember Melissa?) long before we decided to officially begin the adoption process. You may be thinking, *Wasn't that failed adoption experience enough loss for one couple?*

I invite you to walk down this adoption journey with me and watch God's faithfulness unfold, even in the midst of more loss. In these next several chapters I will be pulling from journals and blog posts to share our story.

****

Blog Post
1/27/12
Just the Beginning

Hello. This is a more personal blog to update friends and family on where we are with our adoption process. Because we have never done this before, I have no idea how often this will get updated. . . . I'm guessing this will start out slowly and pick up a bit after a little while, but from what I'm learning, this is a slow, arduous, and painstaking process. Thank you for joining us on our journey to the Syversen Six.

Background information: When my husband and I met sixteen years ago, we knew we wanted a large family. We didn't know what that looked like, but we both discussed our love for family, children, excitement, and life. We discussed, while still dating, our desire to adopt some day. After we were engaged, we agreed that we both felt adoption would come after we were done having biological children.

Little did we know the journey to having biological children would be a heart-wrenching and painful journey. We were eventually blessed with four biological children, but only after enduring a span of ten years of infertility (with countless infertility treatments ranging from the simple to the very complex) and seven miscarriages. We knew two of our precious losses were little girls.

After successfully having our fourth child, I knew I could no longer bear the emotional turmoil of infertility and recurrent miscarriages. At times, it was truly more than I could bear. With the blessing of my husband, we decided to stop going through infertility treatments and to adopt, which had been our plan all along, without knowing we would face infertility. We jointly decided we would wait for our youngest, Ivory, to reach age three. She is now three and just like a loving father would do, God has moved our hearts towards adoption in ways we could not even begin to imagine or explain.

In December of 2011 God called us—Jason, me, Caleb, and Tiera—to Haiti to assist in the start-up phases of an orphanage on the island of La Gonave, off the coast of Port-Au-Prince (Ivory was too young at this point). While there, I spoke with the pastor we were working with and asked if any of the children at that orphanage were available to be adopted. He told us yes but that they were not a licensed orphanage yet. (Haiti's government does things a little differently than the US. You can apply for an orphanage license, and while you wait, they tell you that you can start the orphanage and will receive the license in due time.) They were looking into transferring two children from the orphanage on La Gonave to a licensed orphanage in Port-Au-Prince. At that point, we would be able to adopt the children.

The meeting for that adoption discussion is February 24 (four weeks from now). The man leading that discussion has told us he will contact us from Haiti as soon as the meeting is over. In the meantime (if that does not work out), we sent in preliminary adoption applications with two adoption agencies in Haiti: Bethany Christian Services and Giving Hope.

Bethany is well known in the US and is responsible for placing over eleven thousand international children with US families. They have an office right here in New Hampshire, only twenty-five minutes from us. Giving Hope was highly recommended to us through a Haitian adoption support group. And the two founders have an extremely impressive record.

Either way we go, there are roughly ten major steps (and with what I've seen and been told, a million small steps in between!) to this adoption process:

1. Preliminary application
2. Formal application
3. Home study and pre-adoption education
4. Begin immigration process
5. Dossier completion
6. Wait and complete additional pre-adoption education
7. Referral of child (we would skip this step if we can adopt from La Gonave)

8. Finalize adoption process in child's country of origin
9. Complete immigration process
10. Post-adoption services

Somewhere in those steps (not sure at all where!) we will need to take two trips back to Haiti: one trip near the beginning of the process and then the final trip to pick our children up.

Also, somewhere in there we need to file for a Presidential Waiver with the Haitian government because the requirements to adopt from Haiti state that adoptive families need to have two or fewer biological children. We, obviously, have four. So, if the president of Haiti does NOT give us the waiver, then all this ends abruptly with no children coming home to us.

On February 9, we are going to attend an information meeting with Bethany Christian Services in New Hampshire. This is just an information meeting. So, for now, we are in a holding pattern until February 24. Our hearts are with those children on La Gonave, so our first preference would be to adopt two from La Gonave. If that cannot move forward, then we are going to move full-steam ahead with another orphanage.

The process can take anywhere from eighteen months to three years. We have friends that just hit their two-year mark and feel it's still a ways off. They are just praying and hoping to have their daughter home sometime this year. But we have other friends who have had it happen in less than a year—and that's all from Haiti.

So, for our first update, we would ask you for your prayers. Prayers for God's perfect plan for this adoption, God's perfect plan for our children (all six), and God's perfect plan for our family.

Prayers will be paramount to this process, and frankly to my emotional state. What I found interesting as I was thinking about it in the shower this morning was that after we had decided to be done with all the infertility treatments, which would also result in no more miscarriages, I cried—a lot! I cried because my heart was so ready to be done hurting and so ready to be done with the twenty-four-hour all-consuming process of thinking about the children that "should've been" and "would this work?" And now I find myself nearly back in that same situation. The unknowns—Will we get the Presidential Waiver? Will we get denied somehow? How long will this take? Are our children well? Will they survive disease, lack of food, a possible second earthquake, etc.?—feel so similar to our struggles of becoming parents thus far.

But, then God reminded me that He is in control. The only control we have is to pray, pray, pray. And then fill out the appropriate paperwork, get things handed in on time, and be on top of what is required of us. Other than that, God is in control.

I'm clinging to these reminders in Romans:

Romans 8:6: "The mind governed by the Spirit is life and peace."

Romans 8:25: "But if we hope for what we do not yet have, we wait for it patiently."

Romans 8:34: "Christ Jesus who died—more than that, who was raised to life—is at the right hand of God and is also interceding [praying] for us."

Romans 9:14–16: "What then shall we say? Is God unjust? Not at all! For he says to Moses, 'I will have mercy on whom I have mercy, and I will have compassion on whom I have compassion. It does not, therefore, depend on human desire or effort, but on God's mercy.'"[3]

My prayer today: "Lord, help us to be governed by You. Help us to do what we need to do, but then to wait patiently, waiting on Your perfect will and timing. Thank You for interceding on behalf of our family—all eight of us. Father, I pray for Your mercy and compassion. Lord, You called our family to adoption sixteen years ago. Now You are bringing us to the crossroads of adoption, and Lord, we are asking You to guide us through it. Guide the government officials on both the US and Haitian sides. Open doors where we do not even see doors. Close doors where there are doors You do not want us walking

---

[3] NIV.

through. Lord, we ask for Your covering over this adoption. We invite You in, Lord. Be our ambassador, be our guide."

****

Blog Post
2/18/12
First Meeting Summary

February 9 has come and gone and so has our first preliminary information meeting with Bethany Christian Services. We have not made a decision to go with Bethany, but it was a helpful meeting to hear firsthand the process and steps we could expect to encounter. Every agency is slightly different and every orphanage requires something slightly different, but it was a good overview.

Jason and I have done a fair amount of our own research already and most of the information was not new to us. For some reason, that provided us both with a sense of security. Often I think people think we have JUST decided to adopt since arriving home from Haiti or on a whim, but that could not be further from the truth.

At the meeting with Bethany, two new countries fell onto our radar: South Africa and Uganda. We have ruled out all of Eastern Europe and South America, mostly because of the costs and traveling constraints. They are so varied and some are so much harder! For example, one country in South

America would require both Jason and me to travel down together, then one of us would have to stay there for two to four months until the child is ready to come home. With small children already in our house, that was not a possibility for us.

To date, we've pretty much said Haiti, but there are complications with Haiti. Most notably is that UNICEF is trying to ratify the Hague Convention and stop all adoptions through Haiti. I don't know all the long-term effects, but I do know that UNICEF believes children should stay in their own countries and should not be adopted outside of their own country. Because of this—and other reasons as well—they have been ratifying the Hague Convention in numerous countries, which has had a major effect on international adoptions throughout the world. We are trying to gather more information on the timing of the ratification. I've read that adoptions already in process and potential adoptions with an adoption decree (I think this comes after exiting IBESR—French, "Institut du BienEtre Social et de Recherches"—basically like the US's Family and Social Services, which vets adoptees, makes sure the adoptions are legit, and that the child is free for adoption, among other things) will not be affected. But, obviously, we are not there yet.

So, I'm trying not to let fear enter in, but we also want to be aware and cautious of the situation. Once in the process, the fees are all nonrefundable and we don't want to get matched with a child only to watch them sit in an orphanage for some unknown length of time— watching them grow up before our very eyes with the possibility that they might never come home.

So, that's where we are. Still waiting, which we will get used to doing. Still praying, which we will get used to doing a lot more of too. Still excited, which we will continue to be throughout the process. The meeting down in Haiti is coming up soon on February 24. We pray for answers coming out of that meeting.

****

Blog Post
2/25/12
February 24 Meeting in Haiti

Hello! I just wanted to give a quick update about the meeting that was scheduled for yesterday in Haiti.

As I told my sister, life in Haiti is so very different than it is in the US. Time moves slowly, traffic is difficult, meetings sometimes happen and sometimes they don't, even if they were scheduled. So many of us in my church refer to time in Haiti as "moving in Haitian time." What that means is this: count on nothing and expect delays. When they say church starts at five, that could be five thirty, six, or even seven. It was one of the great things about being in Haiti—life just seems so much simpler.

Knowing this, I was prepared to not hear anything from the meeting, although we were told we would hear something. And, as I anticipated, we did not hear from the director of Vision International Missions (VIM) who was going to be meeting with the lady who runs the Crèche (a name for Haitian orphanages).

I have complete peace about this. I actually have peace about all of this. I believe God is moving and working and it may not be in the direction we were initially thinking. We have been praying as a family and we have been asking others to petition God on our behalf, too.

Thank you to those of you who have been praying. God is in control and all we want is to be in His perfect will. I am confident that once we understand God's will for this adoption, the process will run so smoothly. I want our children home, but I want His will for our lives more, including the EXACT children He wants in our lives . . . not just any children.

God has already paved the way for us. Now we need to dig into His Word and be on our knees in prayer regarding this adoption (and every area of our lives!).

Thank you for praying, saints. We continue to ask for your prayers.

****

Blog Post
3/12/12
Babies Can't Just Be Delivered on Doorsteps!

We heard back from the meeting that took place in Haiti. The news was what we expected to hear. Jason and I are praying. That's really all I can say right now.

Jason and I sat down the other night to have a long conversation about the adoption process. In this conversation, Jason was trying to tell me that he really wanted to make sure that we were moving in God's timing, not ours. He wanted to make sure that we did not approach this adoption with our own strength but with God's strength and guidance.

My rebuttal was to simply say, "But that still requires us to take action, to move forward with the process. God doesn't just drop babies on doorsteps." Jason informed me that God CAN drop babies on doorsteps and he reminded me that out of the three families we know that have adopted, we know of one case where a baby was essentially "dropped on their doorstep."

Me: "Yeah, but that doesn't usually happen. . . ." O ye of little faith.

All I can say is that God has a sense of humor—and if it's His timing and His will, then surely He knows how to drop babies on doorsteps.

Please be praying, friends. We don't know where God is leading us on this adoption journey, but we want to be obedient to Him. We want to hear His voice and we want all He wants for us.

And reminding myself of all of the *little faith* times mentioned in Scripture:

Matthew 6:30: "If that is how God clothes the grass of the field, which is here today and tomorrow is thrown into the fire, will he not much more clothe you—you of *little faith*?"

Matthew 8:26: "He replied, 'You of *little faith*, why are you so afraid?' Then he got up and rebuked the winds and the waves, and it was completely calm."

Matthew 14:31: "Immediately Jesus reached out his hand and caught him. 'You of *little faith*,' he said, 'Why did you doubt?'"

Matthew 16:8: "Aware of their discussion, Jesus asked, 'You of *little faith*, why are you talking among yourselves about having no bread?'"

Matthew 17:20: "He replied, 'Because you have so *little faith*. Truly I tell you, if you have *faith* as small as a mustard seed, you can say to this mountain, "Move from here to there," and it will move. Nothing will be impossible for you.'"[4]

---

[4] NIV, emphasis added.

My prayer today: "Lord, give me faith as small as a mustard seed. Move the mountains in my heart that keep me from having faith like a child. Help me to see, Lord. Open my eyes to what You have for us and give me the faith to trust You will 'drop babies on our doorstep.' Amen."

****

CHAPTER 9

NEXT STOP: NEW HAMPSHIRE FOSTER CARE SYSTEM

Blog Post

4/2/12

Our Journey to 6 Has Become Our Journey to 7

After three weeks, we can finally reveal the reason for all the prayer requests. When I last blogged on March 12, "Babies can't just be delivered on doorsteps!" that was the first day of a journey that has been exciting and overwhelming. We are very excited to share this with you all:

On Monday, March 12, exactly one week after Jason and I had that conversation about God not dropping babies on doorsteps, God dropped three babies on our doorstep!

I was taking the kids for a walk. We were on our road when my neighbor pulled her car up next to us and began talking with me. She talked about how big our kids were getting and asked if we wanted any more children. I told her about our attempts to adopt internationally and how we didn't seem to be making much progress. Then she asked if we were willing to adopt kids here in the US. I told her yes but gave her the reasons we had looked outside the US.

What she said next blew me away. She asked, "What if I told you there were three siblings waiting to be adopted right now and the state is going to split them up if they don't find an adoptive family for all of them?"

Stunned and shocked, I stumbled over my next few words. We talked minor details, then she gave me the number for where the kids were currently staying. She also called their placement parents and told them I may be calling.

That conversation took place 300 FEET from my front door! God DOES drop babies on doorsteps! God has the most perfect timing. I was amazed that He would allow His glory to be shown, even in the midst of all of our doubt and disbelief!

I walked the 300 feet to our front door and cried out to God, "Seven kids? Is that what You have for us? Is this Your plan? If this is You, You've GOT to make this clear to us!" I had determined I would ask Jason and if he said no, then I would let it go. I would not speak another word of it to him or myself.

Later that night when Jason got home, we went for another walk and I told him. I expected him to say no because this was just crazy talk. Instead, with the most peace and assurance I have ever seen in our fifteen years of marriage, he shrugged his shoulders as if to say *No big deal* and said, "Let's do it. Let's call."

That began a three-week journey (so far) of meeting the kids, Daniel, Justin, and Isabelle, filling out a ton of paperwork, having home inspections, looking at new cars and dining tables, background checks, a lot of classes, a LOT of prayer, excitement, and the fear of the unknown.

We are about halfway done with the process and we are expecting to have the kids in our house sometime in the month of May. They will not be adopted until sometime down the road, God willing. There are still many obstacles to get over, namely, the mother still needs to relinquish her rights, but the kids have been in foster care for over a year now and they are not expecting this to be difficult. We are very much praying that is true!

The kids are so adorable! I cannot post a picture, but they will melt your hearts! There are three. Daniel is four and a half years old, Isabelle just turned three last week, and Justin just turned one in February.

When we met the children at the playground a couple of weeks ago, I had been pushing all the kids (mine included) on the swings. I would tickle all the kids and then give them underdogs. After about ten to fifteen minutes of this, the little girl quietly said something. The current foster mom said, "I think Isabelle's calling you." I responded and said, "No, she's not calling me. She's calling you. She said 'mommy.'" The woman said, "No, she's never called me mommy. She calls me Tata." I said, "There's no way she's calling me mommy, I just met her." Then about a minute later, Caleb and I saw her look at me and we both heard her say in this gentle and sweet little voice, "More pushes, Mommy."

Mommy. Yes, that's what it appears God is saying to us, that we will be mommy and daddy to three orphans. Mommy and daddy to three precious children who so long and desire to be loved and have a stable home. Mommy and daddy to seven children!

We could not feel more privileged than we do. We cannot feel more honored that God has called us to such a high calling. We cannot feel more love for children we have only met once and for children we did not even know existed just three weeks ago.

Our lives have been turned upside down, but we are all in. We have been going through this process at lightning speed because the thought of these children sitting one more day in a home that is not their own is too much to handle. For them to go one more day without a mom and dad to call their own is too much for our hearts to handle.

There will be ups and downs through this. And this is not even a definite thing. Their mother may regain custody of them with some really hard work. But we truly believe God has given us these kids for now and we will parent them and give them the love they need and deserve . . . and we will go to battle spiritually to make them ours. The state does not foresee a problem with the mother, which is why we are moving forward.

Please, we ask for your prayers. We petition you all to take this to God and ask that He works out the details in accordance with His plans, just as we are reminded in these verses:

Romans 8:27: "And he who searches our hearts knows the mind of the Spirit, because the Spirit intercedes for God's people in accordance with the will of God."

1 John 5:14: "This is the confidence we have in approaching God: that if we ask anything according to his will, he hears us."[5]

****

I have to say, it's humbling to go back and read these blog posts. As a Christian, I feel silly that I believed I had heard God or believed He was doing something that He really wasn't doing. Haiti, then *not* Haiti. South Africa, then *not* South Africa. Foster care, then *not* foster care. My only peace of mind in all of this is that we prayed continually and followed all of the threads placed in front of us. If we didn't have

---

[5] NIV.

peace about something then we didn't move forward. If we had peace, then we moved forward.

Blog Post
4/4/12
Home Study Part 1

Note: The agency we began this process with (known as The Agency) was shutting down its adoption division and therefore transferring all of its current cases to DCYF—Division for Child, Youth, and Families. So throughout much of this process you will read about The Agency and DCYF. That's why. It was a mess and not ultimately in our best interest.

Jason and I had our first of three meetings with our caseworker at The Agency to complete our home study on Monday evening. The meeting went well overall, except for the fact that she had not yet read either of our autobiographies and proceeded to ask us both nearly all of the questions that were in the autobiography. Had she read it, we would've been able to cover a lot more in that two-hour time period.

Regardless, the meeting went well. We went over attachment issues, behavioral issues, corporal punishment, and counseling services the state offers to these children and their adoptive families. The caseworker also took a tour inside and outside of our house. She was very nice and we hope and pray she will be a strong advocate for our family.

She asked if we had any questions, so I jumped at the opportunity and asked my main question: could we still lose them to another family if DCYF thought it best they be with another family? It was my understanding (from someone else at The Agency) that once we got placed with the kids and they were cleared for adoption, their files would be offered to other pre-adoptive families. Our caseworker clarified that once the children were placed with us, they would not leave us unless there was a problem at our house. That relieved quite a bit of anxiety I have had over this process.

So, for now, we have another appointment with the caseworker on April 16, and a total of seven classes to attend.

Yesterday Jason and I also went to get our fingerprints and background checks done. Those should take about three weeks to come in. We are really praying Jason's don't take long because we have a friend whose fingerprint results took forever to return. I also had a really sweet moment with a friend from our homeschool co-op when she handed me a bag from Macy's. I asked her what it was and she encouraged me to open it. Inside were two polos shirts, a pair of jeans, and a pajama set—all for the baby. It blessed me more than words can say. When we got home, I showed Jason and the kids and they all cooed over it, then I said, "It's so weird having little boy clothes in the house again."

Thank you for your support and encouragement. Jason and I were really blown away by the support when we announced all that is going on. Please continue to be praying for our family, the kids, and for the process. Thank you!

> *He who can reach a child's heart*
> *can reach the world's heart.*
>
> Rudyard Kipling

****

Blog Post

4/8/12

A True Easter Celebration!

Happy Easter, family, friends, and blog readers!

What a glorious day the day has been! I truly feel that God came down and orchestrated the perfect Easter miracle for our family.

A week ago, I had asked the current foster family if we could meet the kids again. They were busy last weekend so she told me she would contact me this weekend to plan something. She didn't contact me until yesterday, late afternoon. In an email, she asked if she could bring the kids to our house around noon.

We wrote back and told her we would love that, but we needed to leave by 2:00 p.m. so we could go to a friend's house for Easter dinner. We didn't hear anything back until we were leaving church that morning to meet them at our house. I read the email as we headed home. The foster mom said she was hoping we were willing to take the kids for longer, so it wasn't going to work out with our two-hour window. I called her immediately and asked what she meant by "take the kids" and "longer." She clarified that she was hoping we would babysit the kids beginning at noon. I asked if we were allowed to do that and she said yes since we would just be counted as babysitters. I asked Jason if he was okay with having the kids for the whole day, and before he could answer, all the kids were in the van screaming, "Yes! Yes! We do! Please, Mommy. Please, Daddy!" Jason said yes, so I told her yes and we stuck with the 12:00 drop-off.

Without any real preparation (or even clearing it with our friends first) we had the kids . . . for the whole day! They got dropped off in the driveway with no instructions. The foster dad called from his cell phone and semi-jokingly said, "I'm pulling into your driveway. Come get your package." He chuckled, and my heart sank.

Our package? Our PACKAGE? These are God's children, not a package!

We got the kids into the house and they were all a bit nervous and hesitant. We all (overwhelmingly) surrounded them and doted over them with great love, concern, affection, and care. Caleb went to his room and brought down all of his trains and matchbox cars. Instantly, they all loosened up and began playing. Then our kids took Daniel and Isabelle upstairs and their eyes lit up! They were enthralled with Grandpa Syversen's castle and space station that he built for Jason and his brother, Jon, over twenty-five years ago. The Playmobil guys, the doll houses, the My Little Pony's, and so much more . . . The kids were in heaven! What a blessing to see those toys getting a new chance at life with children who so appreciated them. I felt like it was the scene from the movie *Toy Story* where the toys realize they are still wanted and loved.

After that, all of the kids went outside and played on the trampoline and the swing set. Then they came in for a snack, and finally we headed over to our friends' house. The foster kids were so excited to ride in our cars (we needed to take two vehicles because we didn't all fit into one car) and to pass each other on the highway so they could wave to each other in the cars. Our kids loved that too! When we got to our friends' house, there was no hesitation at all. With two more little boys, they all fit right in. They played all day, inside and outside. They ate well, played well, and were the only young children who didn't cry.

They are simply amazing children. Isabelle and I snuggled. The baby, Justin, and I snuggled. Then it was time to leave. We were dropping the kids off at their current family's home. The little girl was very quiet on the way there. When we pulled into their driveway our hearts broke.

I think we could have gotten away without tears, but the moment we heard whimpering from the backseat, Tiera and I began to tear up. We both rushed to unbuckle our seat belts. By the time we got out of our seats and around the car to get to Isabelle, she was in a full-blown cry. Heart-breaking! Heart-wrenching! We had to give them back . . . .

I picked her up and she clung to me. She cried and said, through a quivering and crying voice, "Mama. Mama." I didn't want to let her go. Tiera didn't want to let her go. I held her for a long time. Jason got the baby out and handed him over to the foster parents. He looked at me and whimpered and gave me a sad little face. Daniel seemed fine and went off running in the yard playing with my kids.

The visit was over. We had them for six and a half hours and it was like heaven. On our drive home, I had our three girls in my car, and Jason and Caleb were in the other car. The moment we got into the car, Tiera began peppering me with questions: How much longer? What if this and what if that? Jaidyn was quiet in the back seat. I looked in the rearview mirror and saw her face. She looked somber. I asked her if she was okay and she lightly shook her head no . . . then the tears started rolling. Jaidyn began crying and her full-blown crying caused the whole female car to erupt in tears.

Our hearts hurt for these precious children of God. From that day on, we will be forever bonded with them, even if God never permanently gives them to us. We will pray for them. We will go to battle spiritually for them forever! They just want to be loved and wanted. Our family can provide that for them. Our family can provide so much more for them—stability, security, laughter, safety, parents, love, a Scripture-based upbringing—but they are not ours yet, so we will fight the good fight for them. We will go to our knees! It was the only solace I could give my girls in the car. *Get on your knees. Pray to God! Ask Him for what you want. Go to battle for them!*

We have three more classes, two more interviews, and then we are done with the process. But . . . that's still a month away. So, like I said, we will pray! Please be praying for us!

Thank you, Jeff and April, for welcoming each one of those children like they were our own that day! You mean the world to us!

****

Helpful Hint: If YOU are in the middle of this process and questioning what other people think, remember this:

There were moments here when I thought our friends and family were reading my blog posts wondering, "Is Jason happy about this? Is he really okay with this?" or "Is Bethanee okay with this? Does she really want seven children?" But there was no way we would have moved forward if we were not on the same page. I didn't want seven kids any more than Jason and Jason no more than me. Neither one of us strong-handed or manipulated the other into doing something we didn't want. Neither of us "convinced" the other this was a good idea. God did that. When God speaks, we listen and obey, and that's exactly what we were doing here . . . together.

****

Blog Post
4/16/12
Progress Is Being Made

Hello! "Progress is being made" is such an easy thing to say. It's simple. It's quick. It reminds me of my grocery lists when Jason and the kids are in the car and I tell them I have to "run into the grocery store" and Jason asks, "How many things are on your list?" My response: "Five." There may be five things on the list, but those five things equate to half a cart of food—i.e., fruit, veggies, cereal, milk, and snacks. For a mostly vegetarian family, fruits and veggies are 90 percent of my week's groceries. So, although I may tell him five items, I always walk out with fifteen bags.

Anyway, I digress. Progress has been and is being made.

Easter was lovely, then Monday went by with nothing major. Then on Tuesday evening, a "storm" blew into our home. It is nearly over, though still not in its entirety. With the extreme generosity of my father (who drove down from Maine on Tuesday to surprise us while the kids and I were at our home-schooling coop), our small group, and my dear friend April, a group of twenty-five people descended upon my house! They tore apart four rooms, painted three rooms, and moved a ton of furniture. There is absolutely no way I would have been able to do all of that work on my own, and I feel forever indebted to all of them for all they did. With most of the crew gone by 10 p.m., all the rooms were emptied and painted, with furniture waiting to be set in place.

Wednesday morning, my father and I took a three-hour trip to Lowes to purchase closet organizers for all four bedroom closets (a necessity with nine people in our house!). Upon returning home, I finished all the touch-up painting in all the rooms and my father began on the closets.

Now every room was torn apart and strewn across the upstairs, including and every last stitch of clothing (and whatever else had accumulated in the closets). Thursday brought more of the same, with slow progress being made. As each closet was completed, I found myself in a dizzying act of transferring clothes from one closet to the next and one set of dresser drawers to the next (and hey, while I was at it, I also tackled the summer switchover and the Salvation Army pile!). Wow! What a chore!

By Thursday night, I found mild relief by attending another one of our foster parenting classes with Jason. Five down, two more to go! More progress!

During the class, our group was informed there is a policy of "no more than six children in a home." I made known my disapproval of this policy and of the fact that the agency knew we were a family with four kids attempting to adopt a sibling group of three. This would put us over their limit, and no one had said a word to us about that. The woman leading the class said we would need a waiver to foster and adopt when we already had four children in our home, and that would be determined by a woman at The Agency and DCYF. So, prayers have been prevalent from Thursday night until today in regards to that situation.

Friday morning, the girls and I traveled to Portsmouth and back to pick up my mother, who was joining us, along with my father, for the weekend. Friday, Saturday, and Sunday brought much of the same as the previous days—feverishly working in dizzying circles throughout the whole house. When one room looked as if it were getting close, another switch would happen and it was torn apart again. However, by Sunday afternoon, my father had completed every closet, and with much sadness we said goodbye.

We had warned the kids that as soon as Nana and Papa left, we were going to jump it into high gear and really work hard to have the house picked up and back in order by the start of a new school week . . . and we accomplished that without any tears! Praise the Lord! The new bedrooms are done! The playroom is done! The dining room is done! Now we're just waiting on the delivery of the new furniture, the new hardwood floors (thanks to Rosie, our new puppy, who has destroyed our carpets), and the built-in bookshelves to hold all of the homeschool books that have been displaced from our homeschool room that no longer exists.

Today we began a new week with a clean and very organized home, a peaceful homeschool day, and another home-study interview. Our caseworker came at nine this morning and we went over, in great detail, my upbringing, my life story, my marriage, my parenting philosophy, and so much more. I asked about the "six-kid rule" and she said that was true; however, it should not be a problem with us because of several factors. One, she believes we can emotionally and physically handle seven kids. And two, our house size can accommodate the additional kids without a problem. She told me not to worry about that at all. So, I won't, but I will continue to pray about it.

The next step is making sure all of our references are in, filling out all the last bits of paperwork, Jason's home-study interview on the twenty-sixth, and another class on the twenty-sixth. Our last class is on May 1, and they have said, barring any problems, they really think we will be licensed by mid-May.

So, that's what's been happening this way (oh, and we need to get a new car!).

Again, thank you so very much for your help! Thank you to Lisa Wilson, the Capener family, and the Knickerbocker family for your kind, loving, and generous donations of new clothing and money for clothing for the kids.

Jason and I have been blown away by the love, support, and kindness of our friends. During the interview process today, our caseworker asked me, "How do you feel you and Jason keep your marriage strong?" One of my answers was all of you! The network of support we have through family and friends is so strong and so wonderful! We value it tremendously!

> *We should not be asking who this child belongs to,*
> *but who belongs to this child.*
>
> Jim Gritter

****

Blog Post
4/22/12
A Huge Setback

This past Thursday, our caseworker called and asked to speak to both Jason and me on the phone. My heart sank. I knew what it was about and I knew it was bad news.

Now, let me back up. On Tuesday morning of this past week, I spent time with God during the quiet hours of the morning. During this stretch with God, I journaled this: *God, having children has never been easy for us. You know that. We've had ten years of infertility, seven miscarriages, and a failed adoption of twins (whom we found out on Mother's Day had never existed and the "mother" had been conning us and our church for months). You've seen us through all of it. It's been hard. Very hard. But, we've made it through and because of that, I feel You have prepared us for a hard fight. We will not give up, even if the fight gets hard. We know how to fight for our kids! Give us the strength and endurance to get through any trials that may come up through this process. Amen.*

Two days later, on Thursday morning, our caseworker called and wanted to speak to both of us. We both got on the phone and what I had feared was happening. She told us she had spoken with two women at DCYF (the two managers who make the decisions on where children get placed), and between the two women they had determined there was a new rule (not a law, mind you—a rule) that states no foster or adoptive family can have more than six children, no exceptions.

No exceptions. No waivers. Nothing. With some man-made, large government, state-run DCYF board, they put out a new blanket rule that says a loving family willing to take in three orphaned children cannot have them because we have too many children already.

I sat silent on the phone. I could barely comment. I was holding back tears and refraining from saying something I might regret. Jason jumped into action and got mad. He never yelled, but he stood his ground and pounded her with questions. He asked her, "So, what's going to happen to these children then?" The response infuriated us. We were told that the children would be posted to all the statewide agencies and if no one was willing to take them they would be split up. Split up! Here we sit, a willing, loving, caring family wanting them, already loving them, and we are being told no with the knowledge that they may still be split up. We were livid. It was infuriating.

Our caseworker tried to give us a minuscule grain of hope by saying there was a "possibility" we could fight it. But she didn't want to say more than that for fear of getting our hopes up over something she had no idea how to do or what the outcome would be.

So, the conversation ended with us all agreeing that we should still move forward with getting licensed. Without our license, we have no hope. No chance at all. Once we are licensed (roughly two and a half more weeks) we will work on our options.

Now, even through all of this, Jason and I have remained steady minded about the fact that these three children may not be the children God was intending for us to have. They may have been the catalyst to get us to turn our eyes in the direction of state foster care. So, we still keep that train of thought; however, we will not give up the fight for these kids unless we hear God telling us to stop the fight. We will not give up on them. They need someone to fight for them, their lives, their stability, and their future. So, unless we hear otherwise, we will fight for them.

Jason and I have worked with New Hampshire State Representative David Bates several times, and Jason has had several conversations with Governor Jeanne Shaheen. After we are licensed, we will contact both of them and fight the state on this "rule." We want them to understand how their rules greatly affect the lives of the children and people they represent. Seven children may not be for all people, but seven children to the right family is worth it. How could they not see that adding these three children to our four children is better than splitting the poor kids up? Haven't their lives been difficult enough?

Please be praying for us. Please pray on behalf of these children.

So, while the weekend has been hard coming to grips with the reality that there will be another fight to bring children into our home, we trust in the God who has led us here. We trust in God's plan and we will walk this path, through the storm, because storms always end and on the other side is a rainbow and greener pastures.

Our hearts hurt, but our spirits are not broken.

True, if you fight, there is always a chance you might lose.
But if you do not fight, you can never win.

Taylor E. Bennet

Love until it hurts and when it hurts, love some more.
Love until you don't care about the pain, until you stop expecting
anything in return, until all that matters is loving that person the
best way you can.

Author Unknown

****

Blog Post
4/29/12
Update

Good Sunday afternoon. I wanted to send out a quick update.

Thursday night, Jason and I had our sixth class (out of seven). We discussed the issue at hand with a couple of the social workers there and they were able to help give us some advice and direction.

Friday, Jason had his interview with our caseworker. I was away at a homeschool conference, but he says it went well.

All of our paperwork and references are in now. We just have to wait for our last class on Tuesday night. Assuming all goes well with all the paperwork, Jason's fingerprinting and background checks, and our home study, I think we should have our license a week or two from Tuesday. I'm not exactly sure how long the final process is on their end.

So, the advice we were given was to contact DCYF to inquire about the situation with the kids, specifically the DCYF caseworker that is assigned to the kids. We were also told to contact the Court Appointed Special Advocate (CASA) worker and the Guardian Ad Litem (GAL) worker that is assigned to them. So, we will begin working on that this coming week.

While I was away this weekend, I felt a very strong sense from God that I need to gather friends together to pray. This would not just be for us and our situation, but for all adoptions, all children in need of a better situation in their lives. I will be getting more information out on that when I organize it in my mind and on my calendar.

The Gift of Life

I didn't give you the gift of life,
But in my heart I know.
The love I feel is deep and real,
As if it had been so.
For us to have each other
Is like a dream come true!
No, I didn't give you
The gift of life,
Life gave me the gift of you.

Author Unknown

Thank you for the prayers you all have been lifting up on behalf of these kids and our family. We truly appreciate it.

****

Blog Post
5/5/12
"No Amount of Prayer Can Change This!"

What a ride! Up, down, up, down—but we are not weakened or broken. I write to you several days after having a conversation with our caseworker. She informed us that NO amount of prayer will change the rule. We were told there is a lot of "political" stuff going on behind closed doors. The social worker for the children talked to our social worker and said, "My hands are now officially off this case. I'm not touching it." Our social worker has no idea what happened and why the other social worker said that, but she finished our home study anyway and made note that we still wanted these three kids.

And we prayed. As a family, we discussed that maybe this really is God closing the door. We are starting to feel there may be an end to all of this, but for now, we still pray for these three children and their mother. Maybe this is the reason God has them in our lives—to be praying for their mother.

We were supposed to attend our last foster parenting class on Tuesday night, but we were unable to make that class, so we have a new date of May 21. After the class, we have approximately a two-week wait. So, we should be licensed in about one month. We were told to expect a lengthy wait before we get any children, so it may still be a while before we are placed with these three . . . or any children at all.

You can do more than pray after you have prayed; but you can never do more than pray until you have prayed.

A. J. Gordon

Thank you for your prayers. They mean so much to us!

****

Blog Post

5/31/12

You Don't Want to Miss This One!

We are licensed to foster and adopt!!! The news just came in about thirty minutes ago.

So, thank you ALL for your prayers! We are licensed, but the battles are not over. The enemy is not happy with what we are doing—giving children a loving, Christian home—and he wants to stop us from adopting a sibling group. He doesn't want God's love, truth, and light to be given to anyone, certainly not little children whose spirits and lives God cares about so much. The enemy tries to keep us from God, but God's will is for us all to come to know Him, make Him Lord of our lives, and then tell others the good news of the gospel.

Thank you! Thank you! And thank You, God!

****

Blog Post

6/8/12

No Compromise—Waiting in Prayer

Wednesday we met with The Agency and the placement coordinator and her supervisor. The meeting did not go well. They wanted nothing at all to do with hearing about the bill or about any families we had located that have been placed with children that put them over the six-children limit. The super-visor snapped at us and stopped us dead in our tracks.

We were re-informed, for the tenth time, that "our" chil-dren are not free for adoption yet and that they won't even be available until August. Then the parental rights have to be terminated, which could take until December. That was six months too long.

We went back and forth on why we joined The Agency and what we are NOT interested in, as well as what we are inter-ested in.

We told them we are still not interested in doing foster care, respite, or emergency placements. We are only interested in getting an answer about these three children. We also said that while waiting on these children, we are willing to hear about other sibling groups whose termination rights are already in the process of being terminated and who are therefore being freed up or are currently free for adoption.

After leaving the meeting, I was very, very frustrated. As I was climbing into the car, our caseworker shouted out to us. I turned around to find her walking over to our car. We got out and she asked how the meeting went. I told her not well and her response was this, in a whisper, "I'll have to call you. I was told I wasn't allowed in that meeting." *What?* She's our own caseworker and she was told she wasn't allowed to be in there? Jason became pretty upset after hearing that.

For now, we're waiting it out. We will continue to be praying and waiting on God. We don't feel a release to stop fighting for these kids. We have the names and numbers of many workers at DCYF—people who have been involved with getting families placed with large sibling groups that put them over the limit.

We will begin contacting them ASAP. Thank you for your continued prayers!

We found out on June 21 that the state was looking for a pre-adoptive family for the kids. I went into "Mama-bear protective mode." I began digging deep into every contact we had and into every name we had been given. I was relentless in placing phone calls. I was relentless in praying and crying out to God. I tracked down people from all over DCYF throughout the state. I was becoming hopeful, not that we were going to be given the children, but that we would have a fair shake at getting placed with the children.

I had so many long conversations and I was told, "Bethanee, I am personally seeing to it that your portfolio, which I have here in my hands, will be on that table and will be a serious contender as a pre-adoptive family." Outside of contacting the governor, I felt I had done everything I knew to do. The rest we had to leave in God's hands.

> *Whatever happens, conduct yourselves in a manner worthy of the Gospel of Christ.*
>
> Philippians 1:27 NIV

****

Blog Post

6/21/12

It's Official. They're Being Moved—Prayers Needed!

My heart is breaking. I know I should be happy and excited because there is movement, but I'm not.

The current foster family has officially placed the three children back into the New Hampshire Foster Care system. Meaning, the family has officially said they no longer want the children.

We need prayers!

We were told that on July 5 the DCYF will take home studies from all over the state of New Hampshire and they will consider anyone interested in these three children. Our information will be included in the matching meeting, but we've been told our chances are extremely slim given how many children we have.

I would be lying if I said I was okay. I'm not. I'm scared. I'm really afraid we will not get them. This is it. This is the final say. On July 5, we'll know if the state gives them to us.

Even if they give them to us, they are not free for adoption yet, but the state giving them to us is the biggest hurdle, in my opinion. And I keep reminding myself of this verse from 2 Timothy 1:7: "For God did not give us a Spirit of fear but of power and love and self-control." (NET) July 5 is the second biggest day for our journey with these children, second only to the day when we go to court to make their adoption official. If the state of New Hampshire and DCYF decides not to place them with us on the July 5, then it's over.

I know this is all in God's hands either way, but I am asking you all to be praying. I'm asking you all to be putting us on your prayer lists. We love these little children so much and our heart is to give them the adoptive forever family they need and deserve.

On Friday, June 22, we got some more news about the kids that nearly broke my heart. We found out friends of ours had put in to get the kids too, knowing we had been trying so hard to get them. I had to leave the house and cry. I poured my heart out to God and I had to fully surrender my heart and the kids to the Lord. I needed to cry out loud and tell God that no matter what may come, I will serve Him and praise Him.

> *And the peace of God, which transcends all understanding, will guard your hearts and your minds in Christ Jesus.*
>
> Philippians 4:7 NIV

As I drove away from my house that day, I played Bethany Dillion's song "Hallelujah." Tears poured down my face as I sang the words to her song, "Lord, whatever's in front of me, I choose to sing hallelujah!"

So, I surrendered the kids—and my heart—to God. Peace has slowly been taking up residence in my heart and mind. I am so thankful to God for that. That's not to say this has become easy, but I believe now if we don't get placed with the children I will, with time, be okay. I'm praying God will give my children the same peace. With the most recent news we had received, my kids were so hurt. They were crying and confused, so I continue to be praying for them.

****

Blog Post
7/2/12
A Heart Surrendered, a Conviction of Faith

Recently I sat quietly having my time with God and I was encouraged by God's faithfulness and timing.

I read the story from Numbers about Moses and Aaron leading the Israelites to the Promised Land. Joshua and Caleb were sent out to see what the Promised Land was like. When they returned, they told Moses and Aaron about a land flowing with milk and honey, a land with powerful people and giants. When the Israelites heard this, they were afraid. It reminded me of the song I sang as a new Christian, "Giants in the Land" by Grover Levy. The lyrics say, "Though there be giants in the land, I will not be afraid. He brought us out to lead us into the Promised Land." And though there may be giants in this situation, I will not be afraid. I will move ahead, bold and confident. Taking every step in obedience. And that is exactly what I've done.

I told Jason, "I feel like David. Just as he prayed diligently and fasted for God to spare the life of his child, so I have prayed and done the very best I knew how, to be sure we will be fairly considered for these children. That's all I can do. Now we continue to pray, fast, and wait on God. If we are not placed with these children, I will not look back with regret, wondering if I did enough, beating myself up with guilt and regret wondering if I fought hard enough for them. I will be able to accept it, not without shedding some tears, I'm sure, and I will be able to move beyond the pain and look for the ways God intends to expand our family through adoption."

So, as for the information I have to date, there are several families in the pool for consideration. God has to make this happen.

Thank you to those of you who have been supportive throughout this. You have no idea how much your support has meant to us. Thank you!

****

Blog Post
7/7/12
Praise and Peace

Praise and peace—that's what we have. I knew God was in control and I had peace as I read over these verses:

Psalm 13:6: "I will sing the Lord's praises, for he has been good to me."

Psalm 16:7: "I will praise the Lord, who counsels me; even at night my heart instructs me."

Psalm 28:7: "The Lord is my strength and shield; my heart trusts in him, and he helps me. My heart leaps with joy, and with my song I praise him."

John 14:27: "Peace I leave with you; my peace I give you. I do not give to you as the world gives. Do not let your heart be troubled and do not be afraid."

Proverbs 14:30: "A heart at peace gives life to the body."[6]

Yesterday we spent the majority of the day out. Two of our kids had their F.I.R.S.T. Lego League competition demonstration, then we had errands to run. Afterward, we went out on a date with friends. We had a lovely day.

We were expecting a message from DCYF (based on other information we had) when we arrived home. So, when we finally arrived home at eleven last night and saw our voicemail light flashing, I knew it was an answer from DCYF. Jason was working on getting the kids upstairs and in bed. I took a deep breath in, prayed that God would continue to fill me with the peace I had been feeling since last week, then pushed Play.

---

[6] NIV.

It was DCYF. We were not matched with the kids.

The woman who left the message said there were "many" families trying to get placed with these children. We know nothing more. We do not know if they went to a Christian family or not. So, we continue to pray for these children, that God would make Himself known in a real and personal way to them.

When I gathered the family together in the kids' room last night, we shared the news. I said, "This is good, guys. We prayed for God's will—not ours. And God did that. He has different plans for us and for those children. I'm happy about that." Jason said, "Me too. This is what we prayed for." Caleb and Tiera concurred, Ivory was half asleep, and our sweet little Jaidyn cried. She has such a tender heart!

That's it.

We really are in a good place. Jason and I have discussed "what's next" and we haven't come up with an answer yet. We will not go for three children again. We only tried to adopt these three children from the very beginning because we were told they were going to be split up. We have since learned that that is not true. There were many families willing to take three small children.

So, we had to put our name into the pool of other couples looking to adopt one to two in our very small local area. This also meant that we would be constantly compared to our very close college friends (different friends than the ones who had put their names in for Daniel, Isabelle, and Justin) who were trying to adopt more children too. And we would never want to do that to our friends. We love them so much and we want to see them get the children they have been praying for. For now, we are content with four children.

I praise God for this mindset. Two weeks ago this would not have been the case. God is faithful and good.

So, we are just going to wait awhile and pray about it. We may pull out of the foster-to-adopt system altogether (we had other issues with this too and honestly, that's been harder for me than not getting the kids). We may go with international adoption again, or we may just decide we are done and move on with life.

God knows our desires, and in the meantime, we will honor, serve, trust, and obey Him.

Thank you all for your prayers and support.

> *Grace and peace to you from God our Father and the Lord Jesus Christ.*
>
> 1 Corinthians 1:3 NIV

****

CHAPTER 10

SOUTH AFRICA FOR THE WIN

Blog Post
3/26/13
Fifteen Months Later, and a Country Has Been Picked

After everything ended with the sibling group, we decided to go back to our original plan of international adoption. And after fifteen months we have picked a country and we have an agency!

The decision has been very difficult. Since our last decision to adopt internationally, we found that corruption was quite prolific among international adoptions. We interviewed dozens of agencies, went to agency review boards to gather more information, extensively researched each and every agency—which revealed alarming results in many of the agencies. We really needed to pray about whether this was the direction we should keep going. And with zero calls from DCYF for a child to adopt, and with our hearts just not letting go of this option, we revisited international adoption every few weeks with a sense that we were not supposed to stop. We continued praying, reading adoption books, and researching.

All that being said, we feel good about our decision. We are ready to begin walking down this road. A road we are quite certain will be hard (we've already seen that with the foster children we were supposed to get!). But, we feel good. Confident that we have prayed, researched, and talked with friends who have done international adoptions and have a good finger on the pulse on how to proceed and what to expect.

So . . . our country is **South Africa**.

Please be praying for our family. We would greatly appreciate it!

****

I had previously been doing a lot of work raising awareness about human trafficking (sex trafficking, labor trafficking, debt bondage, child soldiers, child labor, and so many more), so I was aware of the risks of child trafficking for the purposes of adoptions. *Yes, this really happens.* In fact, we had read investigative and criminal reports of children being trafficked with international and US connections. We were very uneasy with this. Actually, more than uneasy, we did not want to be unwilling participants in the exploitation of a child. Traffickers will give money to a child's family, allowing the family to feed their large number of children for two to three years, in order to secure an infant or toddler for a Westerner to adopt. It sickened us.

As we read through these reports, we were finding more and more stories of Vietnamese, Ghanian, and Ugandan children who were being bought, secured, and listed as *abandoned and orphaned,* which was only half true. They were abandoned when sold by their parents, but they were not orphans. I read stories of infants and toddlers being kidnapped and brought in by traffickers, who told the orphanages they found the children abandoned. China's and Russia's adoption programs were rife with corruption (some reports stated a couple should bring five to ten thousand dollars in bribery money alone), and we just weren't willing to cross that bridge. We felt way too personally convicted about this to move forward with any of those countries (and others). So, after a lot of research on the topic, we felt South Africa was our safest bet.

If you've adopted from some of the countries I mentioned, I mean absolutely no disrespect. This was just a very personal decision because of the work I was doing and the information I knew. Not all adoptions from those (or other) countries are corrupt. We just didn't want to take that risk.

Helpful Hint if you're walking into international adoptions:

Let me encourage you to look deeply into where your child has come from. You can even hire a private investigator (PI) stateside who will fly to your country and trace the family origin of your child or children to be certain they are, indeed, truly orphaned and haven't been exploited by a trafficker. I read several blogs where couples had hired a PI just to find that their child, whom they were actively trying to adopt, had a family and a good life but was exploited or kidnapped.

One American family was so personally convicted that they even went as far as to finalize the adoption, then on their trip to pick up their child, they actually drove the baby back to his birth family's house, with the help of the PI, and handed the baby back to the birth family. The parents and siblings sobbed hysterically when they saw their little baby. While I can no longer find that article, I would encourage you to read an article from The Atlantic *titled "Kidnapped and Sold Inside the Dark World of Child Trafficking in China" (July 2013) so you have a better understanding of what I'm talking about. This is a real problem and we wanted nothing to do with it!*

****

Blog Post
1/22/14
Love Is an Open Door

The last time I posted, we had decided to go with South Africa as our country. To make a long story short, South Africa received our application and our letter listing the vast array of disabilities we were willing to accept. Some were fairly extensive, including blindness, deafness, missing limbs, fetal alcohol syndrome, babies born to HIV positive mothers but who are not HIV positive themselves, and many more. South Africa came back to us telling us that our list of disabilities was not extensive enough. We were told it was unlikely we would ever be placed with a child since we were not willing to take a child with ALL those disabilities simultaneously. They told us to look elsewhere—at a different country. We were shocked.

We spoke with our agency in New York and they told us no other country they represented would be a fit for our family because we already have four kids and want to adopt children younger than Ivory, who is five years old. Again, more shock.

They had no problem taking our deposit to represent us. They had no problem taking our money for a two-week representation, and now they were turning us away. Shocking! So, at that point, my husband and I said we were done. No more international adoptions for us. For now, we are licensed through the state and we'll see where that takes us.

Well, the whole South Africa turn of events happened last winter. Last winter! It was March of 2013 when we picked South Africa and it's now the end of January 2014!

So, what's been happening since then? Nothing. The state has called us at least two dozen times about taking more children, and they put our name in several more times to be matched, and still we have no children. Every time, the children get placed in a home "with less children." We have turned down a couple of cases because the children were too old. They were older boys and we had made a decision to protect our little girls by not bringing in children older than them.

About a week prior to this past Christmas (2013), one month ago, we received two things: our renewal paperwork for our foster care license and a call from the state asking us if we would like to be considered for three children. Someone within the state system read our portfolio and "fell in love" with us. They loved our family so much that they immediately went straight to work on getting a waiver. You know, that elusive waiver that we were told could not be given to us in the beginning of this whole state foster care process. The same waiver that, when we were trying to adopt the three other siblings the state turned us down because we "had too many kids" and they "couldn't get a waiver because those are held for special circumstances." Yup, that waiver. Regardless, we were excited that we were being considered for a sibling group again. The kids are one, two, and three years old. Two boys and one girl. Exciting! Scary!

It's been two and half weeks since we last spoke to them about these children (and a second sibling group) and we've heard nothing. It's been silent. Not an email. Not a call. Nothing.

Everything in my flesh wanted to call the state and ask them *Why? When? What?* But, in some very tender yet determined moments with God, I heard Him repeatedly tell me not to call. "Trust in Me. Rest in knowing that I have your adoption in control. Do not call." So, I have not called.

Friday night, at our church, we had a night of prayer and worshipping God through music. I heard the Lord speak to me to pull out my journal and just begin writing. In that time with Him, I clearly felt Him releasing me to call. So today, I called DCYF. I got their voicemail and now it's just a waiting game again.

Our license expires in March, less than two months away. It is good for two years at a time. This is slightly depressing to me, but resting in God is such a good place to be. I would be lying if I said this has all been easy and has not caused any heartache, but we continue to pray. We constantly pray. We ask God to close doors and open doors and that is what we have to trust in. And that IS what we trust in.

We have decided that we will not renew our state foster care license.

In the meantime, it's possible God is giving us some opportunities in Arizona. We are not sure, but we have recently had two friends tell us about the adoption pleas coming out of that state. After our license expires, then, and only then, will we look further into this.

So, that is where we are at. We're entering our third year since we began the adoption "process" and we are not one bit further along now than we were then. Thank you for any prayers.

****

CHAPTER 11

{Almost} Home

Blog Post
2/10/14
To Be, or Not to Be, That Is the Question

Last week we heard back from DCYF. They placed the children with grandma. While we feel happy they were kept with family, we feel sad and uncertain about their future. It's a story that's not ours to share, but please be praying for those three sweet little babies. They are unknown to us but known to God. They will most definitely have a difficult road ahead of them.

While on the phone with DCYF we were informed that the other sibling group of three was split up! Every single child was placed in a different home. Our hearts broke to hear this. We are a home willing to keep three young children together and yet they chose to split them up. We were also told the sibling set of two was placed elsewhere, and they had no information on the other sibling set.

(Just in case you're counting, that was four sibling groups that came and went without an opportunity at our end to consider adoption.)

Also while on the phone with DCYF, we were asked if we wanted to be considered for a single boy. He was just under two years of age with bright blond hair and blue eyes. His rights are in the process of being terminated now, so he will be free for adoption soon. This seems ideal to Jason and me as this is what we had been originally envisioning—a single male child younger than Ivory. We were informed that they are only considering our family and one other family.

DCYF will have interviews with both families. After the interviews are complete, they will determine who the young child will be placed with. Our interview is February 21.

Please be praying for this interview. We fear not. We know this is all in God's very capable and loving hands. We simply ask for prayers for wisdom, guidance, opened doors, closed doors, and for this young child who has already experienced great loss. We do not have any other information on what happens if we are picked. That will come in time. Thank you for your prayers.

I have to say, when we decided to be done having children biologically because the mental anguish of going through infertility and recurrent miscarriages was too much for me, little did I know the journey to adoption would look much the same. It's been filled with tears, many prayers, unknowns, loss, peace, and finally an answer to prayer. We have looked back on all that we went through to have our four miracles and we KNOW God knew exactly what He was doing. There was no mistake on His part. These four children were meant to be in our home and we cannot imagine life any other way.

That fills me with joy when I think about the final outcome of our adoption. We will know God had a plan for that child. I do not, under any circumstance, believe that children were born to another woman for my gain, but I believe God will have known the circumstances of that child's life long before anyone else did and will have begun to put things in motion to find a good, loving, and safe home for him. In our home, that will be a home where that child is taught just how loved they are— not by us, but by a heavenly Father who sent His Son to die for us. That child will be taught all about their loving Creator and Comforter.

Blessings.

****

Blog Post
2/22/14
Could This Be It?

Yesterday morning at nine we had our meeting with DCYF. The meeting went well and lasted for about one and a half hours.

We learned more about the little guy. We discovered that he currently arises for the day at 4:00 a.m. and goes to bed around 6:00 p.m.—that will have to change very quickly in our household! There are some normal toddler issues that will be worked out with a different parenting style, but all in all, parenting him sounds very doable.

The first Termination of Parental Rights (TPR) hearing is March 5. DCYF is meeting with the other family that was picked (it's between us and them) next week on February 27. That's a Thursday and the director is not in on that Friday. I informed them that my birthday is Sunday, March 2, and if the answer was no and we were not picked, that I didn't want to find out on my birthday. So they said they would call instead on Monday, March 3, with a final answer. The reality is that my birthday is a Sunday and they wouldn't have called anyway, but I wanted to ensure a pleasant day!

If we are picked, they are not looking to place him with us immediately, doing it slowly. He's lived with grandma since he was taken from mom when he was seven months old. So, we will begin slowly getting him used to us with visits out in public, then visits to the house and so on. That will lead into a permanent placement in our home. All of that will be done in a relatively short amount of time.

We so appreciate all the prayers and encouragement along the way.

****

Blog Post
3/12/14
The End

Well, I started a post yesterday and didn't get to finish it, and today's post has to be completely different. Yesterday I was going to write that we had not heard from DCYF. That I missed a call from them on Monday and spent the rest of yesterday trying to reach anyone with information on our pending case. To no avail. The day came and went and we heard back from not one person! Not one.

Today I set my feet on the ground and declared in my heart to just rest in peace, knowing that it was still all in God's hands, no matter if we heard from DCYF or not.

I had a pre-planned date with my sweet friend Sam (our pastor's wife), who has been with me through this entire journey. She was at the house this morning when the call from DCYF came in. As the phone rang, I excitedly and sarcastically said, "Maybe this is DCYF!"

It *was* DCYF. The lady on the phone began to speak softly in a very "loving" tone. Overly mushy. Over-compensating for the news I already knew was about to come out of her mouth—the little blond-haired, blue-eyed little boy we had been praying for was not placed with us. She told me all kinds of crap like "We are the perfect family and any child would be lucky to be placed in our family." She went on, "The case-workers loved your family and thought your kids were great," and "I know . . . adoption is difficult. You're a great family." Then she stated, "But, the caseworkers just found a couple more things in the other family they thought were a better match for him."

Sam, my sweet friend Sam, gave me the puppy-dog-eyes look and waited till I was off the phone. Then she asked if I wanted a hug. I said no and tried to be strong. However, she just kept looking at me with those eyes and that face. I turned my back to cut a snack for Ivory, and that's when the tears began to flow. Like Sam has done many times in the past, she offered a warm and sorrow-filled hug.

The tears fell, not so much for the loss of not being placed with that particular child, because we didn't even know him, but because that phone call ended two years of hope. Hope that we would be able to adopt through the state foster care system. Hope that we would someday be parents to a child that needed love and hope and protection. Hope that ten years of infertility and seven miscarriages would be made up for with an adoption.

Infertility stinks! Recurrent miscarriages stinks! And two years of trying to adopt and not being one INCH closer to adopting stinks! Nothing about having children has been easy for us. Nothing.

It's why we have appreciated every minute we have with our children. It's why my heart cannot imagine sending them off to school and not home schooling. It's why the thought of sending my son to school in a year instantly puts me in tears.

I called my mom to let her know and she, too, was disappointed. In our conversation I told her I wasn't sure what we were going to do. I had DCYF pull our license since it expires in two weeks, and now we have a critical decision to make— we can try somewhere else or be done altogether. I told my mom I felt I was done. I just can't handle this anymore. I just want to have peace that we can be done or that we have an adopted child, but being in limbo is not my favorite spot to be, ever!

My mom lovingly said, "Bethanee, I know you are tired. For whatever reason, having children has been such a difficult thing for you two, but I would encourage you to keep trying. Imagine if you had stopped after the difficulty you had with each child. Look at the blessings you have because you kept trying."

She's right. Our lives would be very different without these amazing kids. So, when Jason arrives home from DC tonight, we will talk—again—about what our next step will be.

I keep thinking someone who knows our plight will tell a young pregnant teen about us and it will just be that simple. Or that someone will literally drop a child off on our doorstep with a note, asking us to parent their child. Desperation, I suppose. We never want to see a child separated from their biological parent, but if their choice is abortion or adoption, we'd love to see God work in a way that they knew we were here, waiting to love their child.

Please be praying for guidance for our next decision.

****

CHAPTER 12

NEXT STOP:
DOMESTIC PRIVATE ADOPTION

Blog Post

3/13/14

A New Day, a New Perspective, a New Hope

I was reading a beautiful book on adoption today called *Loved by Choice: True Stories That Celebrate Adoption* by Susan Horner and Kelly Martindale. While I was reading it, God gave me the hope I needed with this verse in Proverbs 19:21 (NIV), "Many are the plans in a man's heart, but it is the Lord's purpose that prevails."

I actually woke up feeling much better. It's amazing what a good cry, time with God, journaling, discussion with my husband, and a solid night's rest will do for you. It gave me the perspective I needed.

Last night Jason and I we discussed "if and/or what." We discussed in detail the two possibilities we had in front of us and whether or not to make phone calls in the morning.

So today I made phone calls to our two possibilities, both private adoption lawyers. And both conversations went very well.

One of the lawyers confessed that we just missed a perfect opportunity to adopt the day before from a woman who was pregnant and in jail. But she said situations like that come up somewhat frequently, so not to worry. The lawyer went on to say that they were in need of families who are willing to adopt babies that are harder to place. I asked what that meant and she said babies with darker skin and drug-addicted babies—which deeply saddened us. We are willing to take either, so she was excited about that.

We are meeting with one private adoption law firm tomorrow and the other firm on Monday. I'm creating a photo album tonight to show to prospective birth mothers and from there we will just see what God does. After two-plus years, we've learned to just roll with it.

****

Blog Post
3/18/14
Attorney Meetings

We met with both lawyers. They are night-and-day different. One is very lawyer-like and the other not so much. One has everything planned perfectly, packets ready to go, business cards ready to go, adoption figures memorized, references emailed out within thirty minutes of leaving the office, etc. The other had none of that.

But they were both kind and gave us the same average time frame: six to nine months. That means baby in our arms, fully and legally adopted within the next year.

Our hope is to make a final decision on which law firm to go with by the end of the week, after we've had a chance to pray and talk to our mentors.

An immediate blessing occurred yesterday when I called DCYF to get a copy of our home study report from our old caseworker. She asked why we needed the home study report. I told her that both private adoption lawyers requested it with hopes that we would not have to go through the entire home study process again.

She even offered in an email to do an update for us, if we needed. I wrote back and told her that's exactly what both lawyers suggested and their update fees were very expensive.

She emailed back to say updating the report for us for free was the least she could do to help us. This saves us so much time and money!

Thanks for your prayers to date. Two-plus years and counting. Feeling like we might be able to see some light, finally, as God keeps opening these doors.

****

Blog Post
4/3/14
We're Rolling

Well, it's done! We signed with a lawyer to start the process of domestic adoption. We have also decided to renew our foster care license. So that meant I had to create two profile books with pictures and short notes and blurbs about our family, fill out paperwork for both DCYF and the law firm, and make sure we covered all of the details. A very eye-opening statement was said to us at the renewal meeting at our home for our DCYF license. The caseworker, who had been our worker nearly the entire time, was an older graying lady. She interviewed us and filled out all our paperwork. She told me we would be renewed and good for another two years, but as she was walking out of our house she said, "You know, you will likely not get placed with any children. I do not believe in large families. I don't think families with a lot of children are capable of adequately caring for or loving so many children."

We were shocked! That answered all the questions we had regarding why DCYF never placed any children with us. It all boiled down to one caseworker who was against large families. It was truly shocking to us. [We have since filed a formal complaint with DCYF but to our knowledge nothing happened.]

Please cover our family in your prayers. We need them.

I continue to struggle with my emotions when people share their opinions on what we should do. Dear friends have said some very hurtful things. And I feel like I have to explain myself all of the time.

Why are we adopting? Because we feel called to. We have always known adoption would be a part of our story and God's plan for our lives. And we are adopting because we believe God calls Christians to take care of the widows and the orphans (James 1:27).

We are filled with hope and excitement at the thought of soon welcoming a little one into our lives.

****

Blog Post
5/18/14
A Phone Call

It was my last day on vacation in North Carolina. My alarm went off at 5:00 a.m. I showered, dressed, packed, and headed out the door for the airport. I boarded the plane and it took off towards home. When the plane touched down for a brief layover in Maryland, I turned my phone on. There was a voicemail from our attorney, Margaret.

She had a six-week-old baby whose mother had decided to put her up for adoption. The lawyer wanted to know if we were interested. We said yes. This simply meant we were saying yes to allowing the lawyer to show our profile to the birth mom. She will most likely read through several profiles before she picks a family.

So, we waited for an answer and prayed daily. A week and a half went by and we heard nothing, so I emailed our attorney. Again, we heard nothing. Two days later I emailed her again. This time I got a response. She wrote back, "Nothing is set in stone yet, but we believe the birth mom is going to pick a Latino family from Florida (the baby was Latino). But in the meantime, there is a new situation that just came in. A new birth mom called to ask questions about adoption but has not signed any paperwork. The baby is biracial. Are you interested?" Again, we said yes.

An hour later I got another email telling us there was yet another new situation. The birth parents came to visit the lawyer saying they wanted to put their baby girl up for adoption. This baby was due September 11 in Arizona so we would have to travel to pick her up if we decided to adopt. They asked if we were interested in this possibility, and again we said yes. Two adoption possibilities all on the same Tuesday!

The next day, Margaret called and wanted to speak to me. It sounded urgent. She had learned some interesting things regarding the last baby and wanted to share them with me. The birth parents considered themselves religious just like us, and they home-schooled their older children, just like us. They had asked their lawyer—who worked closely with ours—to pick the adoptive family for them. With that kind of description from the birth parents, Margaret knew exactly who she would pick: us. Margaret said, "If ever there were a match created by God, this is it! I couldn't believe it when I heard all the similarities." But we still had to be chosen by the birth parents' lawyer too. And I was still concerned about the birth parents changing their minds.

There were other circumstances about their situation that make me wonder if there's a decent chance they will change their minds. Specifics like the fact that the biological parents have four other children, the fact that they consider themselves religious, and the fact that they seem to spend a lot of time together because they homeschool their children.

And there is a lot at stake here. If we are officially picked by the birth parents' attorney after all of the paperwork goes through, then we will help the birth mom by paying her a monthly living expense. This is common with private adoptions. But if the birth parents change their mind in the end, all of that money would be lost. Jason and I are still praying about it. Nothing is official yet and we can still say no. For now, we've said yes, but we continue to do more praying

Will you pray with us? We really want very clear direction on this one. There's so much at stake with saying yes and possibly losing a lot of money and time, or saying no and losing out on something that looks really good.

Thank you for you love and support!

****

Blog Post
5/19/14
We're "EXPECTING"!!!

At 11:55 a.m. we received a phone call from our attorney, Margaret. We have been picked by the birth family and their attorney.

We have been picked!

Margaret told us when the birth mother read through the profiles and got to ours, she began crying. In that moment, she picked our family to raise and love her baby. Margaret also told us the birth parents' counselor read through our profile too, after we had been picked, and emailed our attorney to say, "I wanted to let you know, Jason and Bethanee are a remarkable family!"

When Margaret told us the news, ALL of the raw, broken emotions I felt when we decided not to have any more biological children came flooding back. These were not the emotions I was expecting. I could barely breathe. I could barely speak. I thanked her, immediately got off the phone, and began crying. I called Jason and with a trembling voice and tears streaming down my face, I told him we were picked. He could sense that my emotions were not emotions of excitement.

After some time, I was able to process the emotions I felt in that moment. It occurred to me that this adoption situation is no different than that of us finding out we were expecting a baby. We would find out that we were expecting, then it was a "wait and see" game to see if the new life growing in me would die. In this case, it's more of a figurative "die" because at any moment those parents can change their minds, and we would support them in that decision because she is their child. It would be difficult, very difficult, and we would lose approximately one-third of the money (that's a lot!) we have worked so hard to save up for our adoption. It would put us in a place of not being able to adopt for a period of time again until we saved up again.

I cannot quite describe what it feels like to play the "wait and see" game. Most people get pregnant and celebrate immediately. We learned to treat it like a step in the process. "Okay, we're pregnant, but now we need to make it past twenty weeks. Now the baby is born and alive." This scenario is, "Now we need to wait until the baby is born and see if the parents change their minds." To us it is still the same sense of wanting to celebrate but holding our breath for the bad news to arrive.

So, will you join us in praying for this baby and her family? We truly want the best for her, whether that be with us or her biological parents.

In the meantime, we are "expecting"! We have a little less than four months until this little girl makes her presence in this world. We have four months to collect little girl clothing, get a car seat, stroller, create a room with bedding, and so on, for her. And we have four months to pick out a name—yikes! With Caleb, Jaidyn, and Ivory it took us the full nine months!

Will you also be praying for us (and me specifically)? We know the risks are high of "losing" this baby, so we have been honest with the kids about this possibility. As much as we are trying to prepare them for either direction, we still overhear them saying things to each other like, "Tiera, guess what? I'm going to be a BIG SISTER!!!" This little girl is going to come into a family that has prayed for her and longed for her for a long time now. She is going to enter into this home with six people who will dote on her, love on her, and "fight" to spend time with her. There will not be a lack of love or attention!

* *

Blog Post
6/3/14
How do we pray for this little girl?

My heart has been burdened to write this post after several conversations this week. I have mentioned to several friends that this adoption has a lot of red flags, and that we are mildly concerned that the birth mom may change her mind, to which several people have responded, "Well, then we'll just pray she doesn't change her mind."

I appreciate your support for our family, but we cannot in good conscience pray that prayer. We are here to adopt this little girl only if the birth family still feels they cannot keep her. We are all for birth families staying together if possible.

A friend asked me a good question though. She asked, "Why, then, are you willing to go down this path if you feel there are red flags? It doesn't make sense to me. Why are you willing to possibly lose so much of your adoption money on a situation where the birth mom might change her mind?"

My answer: Because God has called us to it, and if He called us to it, He will get us through it. If this adoption does not work out, He will provide more money! I know that! I know He will! There is not an ounce of hesitation in knowing that He will provide what we need at all times.

For numerous reasons the birth mom chose us because our family seemed to be the perfect match for her. If she changes her mind in the end, that is her right to do so. This is her child. Will it be hard? Yes, very hard, I would imagine. We would lose a baby, four months of adoption availability, and a lot of money if that were the case.

> *It's a safe thing to trust Him to fulfill the desire which He creates.*
>
> Amy Carmichael

In the meantime, we still stand in faith. We are still gathering baby items and still trying to pick baby names. We are deciding where she will sleep and how the kids' bedrooms will need to be rearranged. We pray for her and we pray for her biological family.

We thank you all for your support and we thank you for your prayers. Please pray for the baby's health. It appears as though she may have tested positive for sickle-cell disease, which we are trying to confirm right now. And please pray for her birth parents and her siblings.

But don't pray that her mom won't change her mind, please. I would never want to find out someone was praying

> *The heart set to do the Father's will need never fear defeat.*
>
> Elisabeth Elliot

against me keeping my child. The best outcome that could come from this is that we would show her the love of Christ, that she would find God in a way she has never known, and that she decides to keep this baby.

God will take care of us.

Thank you for your love and support!

****

Blog Post
6/17/14
The Peace Within

I'm not sure what God's doing here, but all I can say is that He has done something inside of me. I have so much peace and joy!

Over what? Ironically, not over potentially getting this little girl, but over the opportunity to pray for this family. Over the opportunity to show Christ's love to them. Over the opportunity to pray for the five children in that family that are not even ours. It brings such joy to my heart and real tears to my eyes to be praying for this family. The vision God has given me for this family is so beautiful.

Also, I've been getting this weird sense that God has been preparing me for the birth parents to change their minds at the end of the road—after the delivery, while we are there. There have been several times, while doing my devotionals, when Scriptures popped out at me and I sense God telling me to hold onto those verses when the time comes.

Maybe they won't change their minds. I have no idea what they are going to do. But if they do change their minds, I know God has been preparing my heart for this, and I have such a peace about it. It's indescribable. Truly. I envision them telling us they are keeping her and tears of joy streaming down my face as I realize that God did exactly what we have been praying for—putting her in HIS best care and giving her HIS best plan for her life with her family. I have no fear when I think about this possibility. It is a joy and a peace that I cannot explain.

> *I believe God has us in their lives "for such a time as this."*
>
> Esther 4:14 NIV

This joy and peace over the last few weeks is so hard to put into words. How can I describe how over such a short period of time, God has turned my heart, which was filled with absolute fear, to a place where it is filled with indescribable joy and peace?

My best answer is this: His presence in my life.

I had a chance to speak to the birth mother today, with her counselor on the call too. The conversation went well. Having the conversation with her made me feel better about the adoption possibility. I asked her what they have told their older kids about the situation. She told me that from day one they have been telling their kids she was pregnant, but the baby in her belly belongs to someone else and she's just carrying the baby for them. They all are okay with that. At this point in their relatively young lives, that's good enough for them. They may have questions when they are older, but this is what the parents feel comfortable telling them right now. In a huge way, that made me feel better, too.

Near the end of our conversation, her counselor asked me if I had any more questions for the birth mom. I told her I didn't have any more questions but wanted her to know that our whole family has been praying for their whole family since the day we found out about them, including the fatally ill grandmother. The birth mom got very emotional and thanked me three times. She said, "Thank you. I need prayer and prayer will make all the difference."

I'm telling you, there has been no greater privilege than this, to be praying for this little girl's entire family. What an honor God has given to us!

****

There were several logistical blog entries after this one, but for the sake of this book, I left them out. They were basically paperwork updates, preparing our home, etc. I mentioned that we picked a name for the baby, but we weren't telling anyone. In one of the posts I mentioned how we made a care package for the birth family. My kids all made beautiful handmade cards, drawing adorable pictures and writing beautiful letters to them. At this point, we were signing legal documents, booking our flights, and trying to find a place to stay once we got to Arizona.

****

Blog Post
8/5/14
Progress Is Being Made!

We fly out to Arizona in three weeks on August 30 to begin the journey of bringing our little baby girl home! Our tickets are booked and the days seems to be crawling by.

The birth mom will hit thirty-eight weeks on August 28. She has delivered all of her children in her thirty-eighth week, and she wants us to be there for the delivery, so we are going out early hoping to arrive in time to watch our little girl be born.

What's tricky is that Jaidyn's birthday is September 1. We asked her what she wanted us to do: go to Arizona and miss her birthday but possibly be there for the baby's birth or stay home for her birthday but possibly miss the birth. We let her know we did not care at all which she picked, that she was our daughter already and she was the most important. But Jaidyn immediately responded, "No, Mommy, you guys have to be there. She is going to be your daughter and our sister and she needs someone to be there to watch her be born." All her heart cared about was her baby sister—not her own birthday. To witness that kind of selflessness in your child is indescribable and still makes me cry. I don't know why God chose to bless us so much with such amazing children, but we are grateful beyond measure!

We are still looking for a place to stay in Arizona with the help of some friends. Between the costs of the adoption and traveling out to Arizona, we are hoping for a free or significantly low-cost place to stay for one-two weeks. Please be praying for this!

Would you also mind praying for these things?

1. That fear will not creep back in. The excitement, love, and joy are there and because of that, I definitely feel fear creeping in that we may still lose her. My heart still knows it wouldn't be a terrible thing for her parents to keep her, but my heart also loves her enormously already.
2. I am struggling with some unsettled emotions regarding people's responses to our situation. There have been some role models, leaders, and friends who have made comments (or none at all) that have really hurt us and made us feel less supported. We're not sure if it's accurate or if it's perceived,

but the hurt has lingered and my heart has, unfortunately, held onto it.

3. Support in general: our biggest supporters seem a bit cautious. I'm not sure if it's because this baby is our fifth child or if it's because we're adopting, or even just the fact that people can't see a baby bump growing and share in that excitement with us. Maybe it's even caution for us, for our sake and our hearts. I don't really know. I just know I've been feeling very lonely lately in this journey and could use some prayers.

I saw this quote today and it really helped me a lot!

> *Not everyone will understand your journey. That's fine. It's not their journey to make sense of. It's yours.*[7]

Thank you, again, for your love, prayers, and support. They really do mean more than you could imagine.

****

Blog Post
8/11/14
Your Love Makes It Worth It All

Yesterday at church, God really ministered to my heart. The service began with singing the song "I Surrender" by Kim Walker. The words to the song deeply resonated with me.

---

[7] www.adoptionsharethelove.com

They resonated with where I was, where I am, and where I need to continue to go.

The words of this song strengthened and encouraged me as I thought about how we've had to surrender to God and walk out the plan He has for us. I thought about how far God has brought me in my faith through our own infertility journey and, specifically, this adoption. I thought about how much faith it is taking to trust God NO MATTER WHAT decision the birth parents make. I just started to cry as I was singing. No matter what the answer is, I know that in the end, His love makes it worth it all!

The message that day was on faith. The young man preaching that day, talked about how we are all faced with situations that really test our faith. How we all come to a fork in the road where we need to decide which direction we are going to take: trust and faith or mistrust, worry, and fear. Jason and I were at that fork in the road. Will we fully trust God who has called us to adoption? Will we be faithful to trust Him, no matter what the scenario is? No matter what the outcome is? Again, I teared up.

After church someone was talking with Jason about the adoption. I overheard Jason telling them all that would be lost if the birth parents change their minds. The response from

> *Now faith is confidence in what we hope for and assurance about what you do not see.*
>
> Hebrews 11:1 NIV

the person listening was, "Well then we'll pray they don't change their minds." I've already shared my thoughts on this response, but here's how Jason responded:

"I don't know if that's the right call. The best-case scenario for this adoption is that through Bethanee and me, they would both come to know the Lord, if they don't already. Through that, they would choose to keep their daughter and raise their children to know and love God with all of their hearts. If we lose all of our money, it will have been worth it to know the seven people in that family are now going to spend eternity with their Creator in heaven. If God still wants us to go through this again, He will provide the money all over again to make that happen."

I was so proud of him.

****

Blog Post
8/22/14
A Baby Shower and an Update

We are waiting for a phone call. We found out this past Wednesday that the amniotic fluid around the baby was very low. Because of that our baby girl is having a hard time growing and maturing. As a result, she was measuring at just around 4 pounds. The labor and delivery doctors were discussing doing a semi-emergency C-section just to get her into a safer environment. However, the birth mom is terrified of having another C-section. She has been talking about it the whole pregnancy. Apparently one of her previous C-sections was really rough and the recovery was long and arduous for her, so she was trying hard to avoid another one. However, not at the risk of losing the baby.

We have a phone call, a text, and an email into Margaret, our attorney. I also left a voice mail with the birth parents' counselor in Arizona.

UPDATE: I just heard from Margaret. The appointment went well and the baby is not in distress. All is well, so the next appointment is Monday. Stay tuned.

In the meantime, my very sweet and lovely small group threw a baby shower for me that day. Tiera was able to participate and really enjoyed being a part of the festivities to welcome this little girl. I knew about the shower and decided I would add some humor to the party, so I greeted everyone with a fake pregnant belly and a can of Diet Coke that read "New Mom." Everyone got a good laugh. I had fun with it too.

The shower was lovely. I'm so thankful to those who planned and prepared for it!

While we're waiting for this little girl, I have been going crazy at home trying to get everything finished and in case we have to leave last minute. I think I'm close. I have her suitcase packed, the diaper bag packed, I'm waiting for the stroller and car seat to be delivered sometime today, and I have the Power of Attorney completed for my parents to watch the kids. The kids' schedules, menu, list of handy phone numbers, etc., are all typed up and ready for my dad.

And I want to brag on my amazing parents. My father, who is semi-retired, is coming into town today and will be staying with my kids from the moment we leave until after we return. My mother, who still works, will join him when we send notice that the birth mom has signed the paperwork. She wants an opportunity to meet her newest granddaughter so she is waiting until we call her. I love my parents. They are so supportive of Jason and me. They have never wavered in their love and support for us. They have always been there. They have been there through difficult times and through joyous times.

So, from the bottom of our hearts, Mom and Dad, Stephen and Linda Dupuis, THANK YOU! We love you!

****

Blog Post

9/4/14

God Speaks to Me [The airplane ride to Arizona] – Part 1

I love airplane rides. God and I seem to have this audible-style communication level when I'm on a plane. I've come to expect it. I've come to look forward to our conversations.

I boarded the plane for Arizona with Jason next to me. We settled in and I pulled out my current book, *The Heavenly Man*. The book is about a poor sixteen-year-old Chinese boy who becomes a follower of Jesus and chooses a life of sharing the gospel throughout China despite horrific opposition. It's a great book! I read several chapters during the first few hours of that flight when I sensed God beginning to speak to me through the young man's story. He wrote about serving time in jail for sharing his faith and how God showed up through dreams and words of encouragement, and even a jailer handing him a Bible, following a night of beatings and torture. God had prepared him for the hard time and also encouraged him along the way with truth and love.

I thought God was trying to get my attention as I read this story, so I pulled out my journal and began writing to God, pouring out my heart. This is what I wrote that day, August 30, 2014:

"God, I'm reading *Heavenly Man* now. I feel You showing me that our adoption is going to be the same.

The adoption is not going to go through in order to further Your kingdom [meaning, share more of God's story to those who are living without Him].

How we respond to this loss could have a huge impact. I pray that's not Your real plan as that would bring a great deal of pain and suffering to me, Jason, and the kids . . . but I truly want Your plan. Brother Yun went through many worse situations and His faith in You grew. His testimony was even more widely spread. YOUR testimony was more widely spread.

So, God, I trust You. I know my life is cushy. I know what little pain I will face in my life will pale in comparison to what he and Jesus went through.

I trust You, God. I fear what You are telling me right now deep down in my heart. A warning for the time we're in Arizona. But I trust You. I trust You, God."

I truly believe God warned me. I told Jason that night as we lay in bed discussing the adoption. I told him what I sensed God had shown me on the plane.

****

Blog Entry 9/4/14
Finding Out – Part 2

We landed in Arizona at 10:00 a.m. on Saturday, August 30. We arrived at the beautiful home where we were staying, so lovingly donated by a kind-hearted older couple who use the house as their winter "snow bird" home. We settled in and I emailed Margaret to tell her we had arrived and to give her our cell phone numbers. She emailed us back and told us she had passed our contact information onto the birth parents' counselor and attorney. We would receive a call when the birth mom went into labor.

When hard times come and beat against our STABILITY, we must determine to HEAR GOD'S WORDS and put them into PRACTICE.

Lysa Terkeurst

On Sunday we woke up, got dressed, and found a wonderful church to attend. We went out that evening and purchased gifts for the family—something we were encouraged to do by Margaret, especially for the children. We found gifts for four children whose ages, sizes, and likes/dislikes we didn't really know, but we felt good about our purchases. I emailed Margaret that night to see if she had heard anything. We never heard back from her.

On Monday, September 1— Jaidyn's ninth birthday—I woke up at roughly 5:30 a.m. I lay in bed for a few minutes and started to get a bad feeling in my stomach. I felt sick. I felt panicked, like I needed to move quickly. I strongly sensed that this was going to be the day we found out we were not getting our baby girl. I sensed God telling me to go check the birth mom's Facebook account—that I would find information on there. I had not been on her Facebook account before doing any type of "Facebook stalking," so whatever was on there would be news to me.

So, I got out of bed, grabbed my Bible and my journal, and went to the living room. I knew I needed to be grounded so I read my Bible first. Then I opened up Facebook and found the birth mom's page.

> *I will not cause pain without allowing something new to be born, says the Lord.*
>
> Isaiah 66:9 NCV

There are no words to describe what I found that day. I found out she had gone into labor on Friday night, the day prior to our arrival. There were pictures of her and her family at the hospital as they waited for the baby's arrival. Then there were pictures of the baby from Saturday morning at five with a caption that read, "She's here!!!! Baby girl is here!!! 5 lbs. 3oz, 19" long." Following in the comment section were many congratulatory remarks like, "We're so happy about your new addition."

There was NOTHING that told me the birth mom was giving this child up for adoption. There was nothing that told me she had EVER planned to give this child up for adoption.

I was breathless. I couldn't speak. It was 6:00 a.m. and I was all alone.

The tears began to fall down my cheeks as I tried to catch my breath. I was unable to. Every inhale produced an even louder cry from within my gut. I knew it was over. God had prepared me on that plane, but it didn't make it any easier. Not one single ounce.

After about 15 minutes I was able to gain my composure and sensed I needed to call my mom. I knew the time difference meant she was awake. I called her and told her what I had found. We talked. I cried more. A lot more. She prayed with me and for me, and for Jason and the kids. We got off the phone and I had peace. It was temporary, but it was peace. It was what I needed to carry me through until Jason woke up. I figured there was no sense in waking him up at this point, so I just let him sleep. But the peace that washed over me from my mother's prayer was just what I needed.

Thank you, Mom. I love you so very much.

Jason woke up around seven thirty and walked out to find me reading Heidi Baker's book *Expecting Miracles*. I was hoping God would somehow change the outcome if only I had enough faith to expect miracles. I really was hoping for a miracle.

He saw I was a mess and asked what was wrong. I began to tell him. He sat in silence with pursed lips. I could tell his mind was racing with thoughts like *How do I fix this? How do I help Bethanee? How has this happened? Where did we go wrong? Did we cause this? Were we off-track? How is there another failed adoption? What's the next step?* I just sat and cried some more.

Jason eventually came over next to me and just held me for a long time. So tender. We both tried to deal with our own anger and our own grief the best we could.

We immediately emailed our attorney, Margaret, in New Hampshire. We kept the email vague because we wanted to know what she knew without telling her what we knew. We wanted to make sure the breakdown was not with her.

To make a long story short, we eventually reached her by phone later that day. We probed her and she genuinely seemed to not know anything. We finally shared our discovery with her, and she was confused and shocked. She wanted a few minutes to look at Facebook herself. She told us she would call us back. Eventually she did. She told us she shared the information with the birth parents' attorney and counselor. They, too, were shocked. The counselor was even supposed to be in the delivery room with the birth mom and myself. She was equally baffled by all of this.

They tried calling the birth mom to get information. At this point we were all fairly certain the adoption wasn't going to happen. The birth mom was not answering her phone. The hospital confirmed she was at the hospital but she didn't answer that phone either. Eventually her attorney was able to reach the hospital social worker, who went in and spoke with her. The birth mom told the social worker that the birth mother's father pressured her to change her mind and she was keeping the baby.

It was 5:00 p.m. on Monday when we received this news. Margaret told us it was over and we were to book our flights home. We decided to call the kids. This was a very difficult call to make, one, because we were so far away and, two, because it was Jaidyn's birthday. We got on FaceTime and had all the kids circle around so they could see us. Before we could even share the news, they started asking questions. "Mom, are you okay? It looks like you've been crying." My voice quivered and I began to tell the kids the news. It was heart wrenching.

Ivory just commented, "All the pumping for nothing, Mom! Now it's all wasted!" Yes, baby girl, it was all wasted. (I had been pumping to produce my own breastmilk by the time the baby arrived). Tiera closed off her emotions to all of us and went and sat in silence in the corner. I knew her heart and spirit were crushed. Caleb handled it just like his dad—very analytically. Jaidyn, on the other hand, began sobbing and was unable to talk or catch her breath. She was inconsolable. It was my lowest point to date in all of this. I began to cry hard. Watching my baby girl hurt so much, especially from the

Tears are the silent language of grief.

Voltaire

actions of others, was torture. I had to ask that someone in the house would please go over and hug her and just hold her. It was breaking my heart to watch.

We ended our phone call in a long prayer. We booked our tickets back home for the next morning—an additional huge cost we were not expecting! We packed, returned the gifts we had purchased for their children the previous night, showered, prayed together, and went to bed.

*God, I may not understand
how everything will work out,
but I trust You.
I don't see a way, but I know
You will make a way.
I have faith that at this very moment
You are touching hearts, opening doors,
and lining up the right breaks and right opportunities.
Things may look dark and bleak now,
but I have faith that
my dawn is coming![8]*

---

[8] www.GodVine.com

****

Blog Post
9/4/14
The Aftermath ~ Part 3

We woke up the next morning, packed up the last of our items, and left for the airport. I struggled throughout the day to not cry. The only thing that helped was to not talk, at all. There were reminders everywhere. Checking in, the attendant asked where our lap child was. We had to explain. On the plane ride, the people I was sitting next to wanted to chat and asked why I was in Arizona. The day was just difficult.

Here's an entry from my journal that morning—September 2, 2014, the day after we lost our baby girl. The sweet baby girl we had decided to name Eliana Faith.

> We lost her. Our little Eliana Faith, gone. She's where she belongs naturally, and for that, I'm happy . . . but the pain I feel for our loss is unbearable. I see reminders everywhere. Parents carrying infants in Baby Bjorns. An empty infant car seat we now have to take back to New Hampshire with us. A full diaper bag. My empty arms.

> God, I cannot understand. I cannot come to grips with why You would allow this to happen again.

I am hurting. I am angry. Satan keeps trying to feed me lies to make me not believe in Your existence, but I won't listen. My heart questions why. Why me? Why us? Why again? WHY? I don't even know how to process all of this.

Jason has been so good to me. He knows how to handle my fragile emotions. He knew speaking to me was hard because it would make me cry, so he just stayed quiet and rubbed my shoulders, offered his hand, gave me frequent hugs and kisses.

After we boarded the second leg of our flight home, I quietly said, "I'm not ignoring you." He said, "After twenty years, I know that. I know your silence is just you trying not to cry and my talking and trying to help makes you cry. I understand that now. I get it."

I love him so much. I love how he loves me.

We arrived back in Manchester late Tuesday night. I asked my dad if he would please bring the kids to the airport. I just wanted to hug them, tell them how much I love them. They were excited to show us a special surprise they had for me: they had thoroughly cleaned out my car. They washed the inside and outside, vacuumed it, and even washed all the windows. They also told us there were surprises waiting for us at home.

We pulled up to the house and found that some dear friends had brought over flowers, a board game, and two cards. And the whole house was cleaned up. While we were flying home that day, Jason had messaged a few friends asking them to come and get all the baby stuff taken down and put away before we got home. I walked into the room where the crib was and saw a perfectly put-together room. Clean, vacuumed, and missing the crib. I dropped down on my knees and just began to cry. Ivory came in and just held me and sat on my lap, wiping away my tears. This time, the crying lasted only a few minutes, maybe in part because kids kept coming in.

In that moment, I was overwhelmed with the great love my husband and friends have for me. Though I was heartbroken and hurting, I was so grateful that Jason realized it might be too much for me to deal with all of the baby stuff so he was thoughtful enough to ask our friends for help. I would have cried my way through every outfit, every pair of shoes, newborn diapers, and hair bows. Even as we arrived home with the baby gear we carried to Arizona, the infant car seat, diaper bag, and suitcase filled with Eliana's clothes were swiftly swept right out from under my nose. I still don't know what happened to those items. They were just gone the minute we walked through the door.

Such love and warmth upon coming back into my home. I felt the kindness of my husband, father, kids, and my friends April, Angela, and Laurie. I will forever be grateful for your love and kindness during this time.

****

CHAPTER 13

THE AFTERMATH AND THE BREAKTHROUGH

Blog Post
9/14/14
The Aftermath Continues ~ Part 4

We arrived home on Tuesday, and on Wednesday morning I spent some time sitting on the deck with my dad. It was beautiful outside. The birds were chirping and the temperature

Hardships often prepare ordinary people for extraordinary destiny.

C. S. Lewis

was a perfect 72 degrees. We eventually moved inside to the breakfast table and as we were sitting there, I heard an email come in on my phone. It was from Margaret.

I grew numb all over again as I began to read it. A new pain. An even harder reality was unfolding before my eyes. I tried to put on as brave a face as I could since my father and the kids were all sitting in the kitchen with me.

Here are a few excerpts from the email:

> Bethanee and Jason: I hope you are home safely by now.

> I am so sorry that [the birth mom] managed to pull what appears to us all to be a scam in front of trained professionals like [the attorney's name] and [the counselor's name].

> As of yesterday, her attorney informed me that the living expenses were paid to the birth family on Aug 29 and when the attorney tried to put a "stop payment" on that check, the bank told her the check had already been cashed on the 29th. When we realized what was happening on Sept 1, I asked the attorney to IMMEDIATELY stop payment on that check and she tried.

> This is a disaster and I am very, very sorry for your loss.

I sat at the table and my dad asked if everything was okay. I briefly told him what was going on. I sat for a few minutes more, then I couldn't handle the pain anymore. I walked upstairs and curled into a ball, hiding deep in a corner in my bedroom. I just wanted to be alone. I started to weep from the deepest, darkest parts of my being. Weep.

That was it. I was hitting rock bottom and I just didn't care who heard me or who saw me. I had tried to be brave for as long as I could, but I just couldn't handle the latest news.

We didn't lose her because her mom changed her mind—that would have been hard enough. We lost our adoption dream because we were scammed. That birth mom never planned to give her child up for adoption. She had a nursery set up already. A name picked out. And her family and friends were all welcoming the new addition. This was beyond comprehensible and well beyond what my already fragile emotions could handle.

All the birth parents gained from scamming us was four thousand dollars. But we lost so much more than that. We lost a future, hope, and life with a new addition to our family. Tens of thousands of dollars that we had worked so hard to save up so that we could adopt. It's all gone. With that comes even more lost hope. This means there can't be another adoption. We have nothing left. No money. It would take a miracle for us to have the funds to adopt again. It would take an act of God, a large donation, fund-raiser or something. We just don't have anything left. And we lost our sense of trust in the goodness in people. This was evil. It was pure evil. For four thousand dollars they wreaked havoc on our lives. For what?

I'm aware that while I struggle with this heartbreaking loss, I have friends battling for their lives in their fight against cancer. Yes, there are worse things that could be happening, but this is real for me. It's what is real for us right now.

After that last, long, really hard cry on Wednesday I've been doing better. I'm hurt. I'm angry, but I still pray for that family.

It's still hard for me to talk to people. I've received several phone calls over the last few days that I have allowed to just go through to voice mail. I'm sorry. I just need time to get to the point where I am not crying every time I talk with someone.

Today I took the kids to the lake and am trying to resume life. Monday I will begin school with them. Life moves on. But it's been hard. Babies are everywhere and it stings.

Several people have asked Jason what we will do next. We don't know. Right now, we are healing.

We have received so many texts, emails, Facebook condolences, prayers, and support. And we are SO thankful to all of you. You all are a blessing to us. Thank you.

****

As I read back over these posts, I realize those were some of the darkest days of my life. Nothing has compared to that level of loss. The emptiness, loneliness, and complete isolation I felt is hard to put into words. People were trying to understand, but there was just no way for them to truly get it. I felt as though they were expecting me to move on with life more quickly, but to me it felt like we had had a stillborn baby. We had everything picked out and ready for her: a name, dresses, shoes, crib and bedding, car seat, stroller, swim suit, coat—everything. I think the expectation is that if you didn't carry the child in your womb, the loss must not be as bad, but it was my worst. After seven miscarriages and two failed adoptions, this third failed adoption was the worst.

Losing Eliana Faith was the lowest point in my life, for many reasons. It was unbearable simply to lose her. And we lost tens of thousands of dollars we had been saving for years, our entire adoption fund, so private adoption was now literally robbed from us. I lost hope in the goodness of humanity for a few months as this experience rocked me to the core. It rocked my faith in God and it rocked everything I had been teaching my kids about God. I questioned, *Is God real? Does He exist? And does He care?* That caused me a great deal of mental anguish. My faith was so important to me and now I was questioning everything.

I needed the comfort of friends and family, but after just a week or two of being home, the calls and texts stopped and the silence became deafening. For weeks I cried. I didn't want to go to church, out in public, or even come down the stairs in my own house. I didn't want to face my husband, who was asking why I was still crying. I didn't want to face friends with babies, and there were several women at our church due at the same time Eliana was due. I didn't want to face the fact that everyone else had moved on except me. I didn't know how to keep moving forward. I was hurting and broken.

****

Blog Post

12/9/14

When You "Get It": It's Not about You

It's been four months since we lost Eliana. I cried for months, just trying to process all that had taken place. I questioned every human being and questioned the adoption process at every level—international, foster care, and private.

My unknown
FUTURE
is in the hands of
the All-Knowing
GOD.[9]

I was disheartened by the people who didn't "show up" when we thought they would, and was encouraged by the "strangers" who did show up when we didn't expect it. Some people didn't seem to care about our loss, or maybe they didn't understand or didn't know what to say. I felt so much hurt and confusion inside of me because that's not how I would have responded if I knew someone was hurting. When someone I know and love is hurting, I reach out to them.

---

[9] www.GodVine.com

I was really battling internally with all of this. Hurt was pouring out of me from every side. Hurt turned to anger, and both emotions just lingered.

I was hungry to get away from everyone and everything. I needed time to just be with God. I needed time to tell Him how angry I was with him. How MAD I was at Him. How unfair all of this was.

You see, this wasn't just about losing Eliana like my husband and friends thought. This was about all of the hurt and pain we experienced through infertility and recurrent miscarriages and failed adoptions. This was about fourteen years of trying to grow our family and suffering one loss after another. This was also about losing hope, losing trust, losing every good and perfect thing I had known of my Lord and Savior. And that terrified me.

Days, weeks, and months passed. I still felt numb to God. I would cry out in the car. I would cry out quietly when the kids were home.

I needed to rediscover, for myself, that God is real. That He really does care for us. That He cares for the details of my life. I needed to fall in love with God all over again. And I needed to hear from God again. We needed to know if we were chasing something that was not in His plan, not a part of His will for our lives. Do we keep plugging away on a plan for adoption or do we call it quits?

Finally, breakthrough came.

Just before Thanksgiving we were matched through private adoption with a little baby boy in Arizona due on December 20. We were matched for just a few days (and only three and a half weeks prior to his due date!) when Margaret, our attorney, told us the adoption attorney in Arizona wanted a crazy amount of money for the adoption—money we no longer had because of the failed adoption, money that made us feel like we were "buying" a baby in a bidding war with other couples. We did not know what to do.

We eventually decided to say no to this adoption opportunity. We just didn't have peace about entering into a bidding war with other couples over this little boy's life. That was incomprehensible to us.

But our plan for adoption meant saying yes, not no. We had been trying for three-plus years to adopt, and now we were being matched again and had to say no.

As I sat on my bed that night and prayed to God, I asked Him to make it very clear if we were to adopt that little boy—or if we were to even adopt at all. I asked Him to make my devotional about adoption. I needed to know there was no chance it could be a coincidence. And this is when breakthrough came!

I desperately wanted to hear from God, so I sat in silence and did nothing—nothing at all. Then, I heard Him speak to my heart telling me to open up my devotional, *Streams in the Desert*, to the entry for that specific day. It was based on Hebrews 2:10 and was about suffering, about how we are perfected through suffering. But it wasn't just about suffering—it was also about adoption. I was in shock. I had to read the entry from the previous day and the one for the next day. They were not about adoption. I scrolled back and forth several days and none of those devotionals were about adoption. Just that one single day was about adoption. God did exactly what I had asked Him to do. I began to cry.

As that night unfolded, THREE friends stepped up and offered, of their own accord, to do fundraisers for our adoption, in addition to another friend who had already set up an adoption fundraising account for us. So, there were FOUR friends offering to help us move forward with our adoption dreams. Then, two more friends stepped forward to help us raise adoption funds. This happened a full three months after the adoption failed—and SIX friends, ALL ON THE SAME DAY, stepped forward and offered to help us raise money to adopt again AFTER I BEGGED GOD to reveal Himself to me. This was God! This was all part of my confirmation.

The breakthrough, though, was not "more babies." The breakthrough was in what God taught me: "It's not about you, Bethanee. It's about the plan I have. It is greater than you can see currently so trust Me. I have something great for you and Jason."

"That sounds so simple, and maybe I'm slow or stubborn, but there was a great peace that overtook my heart and life when I got that lesson. I can now walk into each situation with peace again and say, "Lord, if it's Your will, it will happen. Everything else I will use as an opportunity You gave me to be praying for these birth moms and their babies."

For I know the plans I have for you," declares the Lord, "plans to prosper you and not to harm you, plans to give you a hope and a future."

Jeremiah 29:11 NIV

Maybe out of all of this we will start a nonprofit to help out birth mothers or adoptive families. Maybe we will start an orphanage. Maybe we will fund many projects that will help children. Maybe it will be God opening the doors for me to do what I love, public speaking, and begin to share this story—His story—nationally and globally. Whatever it is, we know God has a plan and that plan is not about us, it's about bringing His love and His goodness and His faithfulness to those who need it. It's not about us!

Breakthrough. Peace. Indescribable peace!

*God has PERFECT
timing; never early,
never late.
It takes a little
patience and a whole lot
of faith . . .
But it's worth the wait.*

*He who forms the mountains, who creates
the wind, and who reveals his thoughts to
mankind, who turns dawn to darkness, and
treads on the heights of the earth—the LORD
God Almighty is his name.*

Amos 4:13 NIV

****

CHAPTER 14

THE STORY OF A LIFETIME

I have not written a blog post for quite some time. A lot of action happened between my last one and the next few blog entries you'll read below. I wrote the following entries several weeks before I posted them. So, as you read these entries, realize things were happening prior to the date they were actually posted to my blog. *Please note: some of the names and locations have been changed to protect the identity of the individuals involved.*

****

Blog Entry 4/27/15
The Story of a Lifetime

Here's a chronological timeline since I last posted in December:

November 25, 2014:

Two days before Thanksgiving, we were matched with a baby boy in Arizona, due on December 20. However, we sensed there were some sketchy things happening with the attorney in Arizona, resulting in a bidding war for his adoption. We felt we needed to back out of the adoption to preserve our integrity and stay true to adopting ethically. This has been critical to us. Critical.

On that same day, a baby boy was born in Massachusetts. This baby, whom I will call Ethan, was placed for adoption with a family in Connecticut.

December 5, 2015:

We received an email from a close college friend telling us about a birth mom in Massachusetts who had given birth to a baby boy on November 25 (this was baby Ethan). She put him up for adoption and he was matched with the family in Connecticut. But that sweet little baby boy got very ill with RSV and the family began changing their minds. By ten days of age Ethan had endured three emergency surgeries for collapsed lungs. Our college friend wondered if we would consider adopting Ethan. We said yes and started the process of introducing ourselves to the birth mom. She asked us if we'd be interested in taking him if the Connecticut family backed out. At fourteen days old Ethan went into heart failure and was in rough shape at a Shriner's Hospital, which was within a day's drive of us. We continued to pray for Ethan and continued to talk with the birth mom about logistics.

December 11, 2014:

At seventeen days old, Ethan passed away. I still hurt for the birth mom, who was grieving another whole kind of loss and betrayal she was not expecting when she placed him in the arms of that adoptive family.

December 13, 2014:

We were at church that morning and I was reflecting on this most recent "loss." Though we never met baby Ethan, we had momentary hope that he would be ours. A hope that was lost.

Yet again, I felt like God was asking me to surrender to Him all my hopes and dreams of adopting. Would He be enough for me if the hope He birthed in us nearly twenty years ago never came to pass? I felt like God wanted me to surrender it all at the altar at the front of our church, so I walked up to the front and knelt before the altar. I prayed. I cried. And I thought about the upcoming year (2015). I realized I did not want to take all of this hopelessness into the new year. I wanted to surrender ALL of my hopes, fears, and dreams to God that day.

Sunday, December 20, 2014:

Exactly one week after I went up to the altar, a series of events began to unfold. Let me set the stage. It was a Sunday. I was home sick so Jason took the four kids to church that day.

While at home, I received a text from the young mom in Massachusetts. This sweet young lady, who was just eighteen years old, had found out she was pregnant again. She said she was thinking of us for the adoption but was conflicted with adopting again because it had ended so tragically the first time with baby Ethan. So, we offered her some encouragement and hope as she walked down this path. We told her we were here for her if she needed a family but put no pressure on her whatsoever.

About one hour later that same morning, I received a phone call from our attorney, Margaret. She had a baby boy for us to adopt if we were interested. He was a drug-addicted baby born in the nearby town of Nashua, New Hampshire. If we were interested, our portfolio and one other family's portfolio would be shown to her. We did some quick research on children born addicted to opiates and decided we would say yes.

The same day Jason returned home from church with the kids. I was still on the phone with Margaret. He kept whispering to me, "There's a situation at church," and I was giving him the "cut-throat" sign to knock it off, thinking he was trying to tell me about some spill the kids caused or some emergency situation at church.

I hung up and told him about the two amazing possibilities we had that morning. He said, "I know . . . I'm telling you, there's a *situation* at the church." Jason proceeded to tell me how someone approached him about our failed adoption last September. This couple knew of a possible private adoption opportunity and asked Jason if we might be interested. Jason gave them a tentative yes. The situation turned out to be TWINS! Twins due in April 2015.

Jason told me to email all of our information and portfolio to the couple he met at church so they could send it on to the family expecting twins. I did it that afternoon. The couple told me the birth parents were unsure about what they were doing at that point, but they were exploring adoption. I told the couple who informed us of this situation that everything was now out of our hands and in their court. I knew if it was God's will, He would take care of it.

Jason, the kids, and I prayed daily for all three of these situations: the birth mom in Massachusetts, the addicted baby in Nashua, and the twins near our home.

One night while lying in bed, Jason told me, "I think the church situation with the twins is going to happen. I don't know why, but I just feel like God is telling me it will happen." Jason rarely ever says stuff like that and he didn't feel that way about any of the other adoptions, including when we flew to Arizona.

Around December 27, 2014

About a week after that monumental day on December 20, we heard back from Margaret. The birth mom in Nashua had picked the other family from the portfolios because they had no children. Again, out of our control—a recurring theme for us.

So now we were down to two slight possibilities: the twins and the birth mom in Massachusetts.

The dates and timing get a little fuzzy beyond this point, but I can still tell you the order of events.

At some point in those days we also received an email from DCYF. I was shocked. We had not received anything from them at all for months. They had a sibling group of three they were looking for a possible adoptive home for. They were hoping we would be an option. I asked the obvious question, feeling a bit of bitterness and sadness creeping back in, "Why now? Why would you let us have three kids now but you didn't three years ago? What has changed with you guys? Because nothing has changed with us."

The answer was a bit disheartening, "Well, there are several big sibling groups and we are just realizing that we could probably place them in families with more children and they'd be okay." Shaking my head, all I could think was "Really?" So, nothing had changed . . . they just needed people.

Regardless of our disapproval of the foster care system and how broken it really is, we thought, *We need to pray about this. These children still deserve our prayers and consideration.*

While praying about this, I received a text from the young mom in Massachusetts (I'll call her Lexi). She had been having some complications so they had run blood tests and an ultrasound on her. She was around five weeks pregnant. At that ultrasound they found something remarkable: TWINS! Twins due in September!

My dear college friend Kelly, who told us about Lexi, texted me when she heard about the twins and said, "Bethanee, I hope God knocks your socks off in 2015!"

And our attorney, Margaret, called that day and told us about a birth mom due in April with a boy.

At this point, we were laughing and having a real, but not serious, discussion about the what ifs. What if we said yes to all situations hoping to get just ONE situation to actually happen? This had been our track record so far.

We added up all of our adoption possibilities that day: 2 local babies + 2 babies in Massachusetts + 3 siblings from foster care + 1 baby boy = 8 new kids!

We had gone long stretches with absolutely nothing. Now, we had to pray about and decide what we were going to do about four different situations involving eight little lives. Real situations. Real families. Real children. Real people.

After spending time in prayer as a family, as individuals, and as a couple, we felt we knew what God was asking us to do.

Both of the twin situations were personal connections. They

were both presented to us on the same day—exactly one week after I surrendered to the Lord and handed it ALL over to Him at the church altar. So, these opportunities were the clear answer to us.

The other situations still involved the "system." DCYF, in our opinion, could not be trusted. We could say no to all other situations and lose them permanently and walk down the path with DCYF for those three kids and find out the state would do the very same thing to us they had done three years ago. The risk didn't seem worth it, not with our current situation. And the private adoption opportunity with our attorney would be an easy placement for other couples waiting on the list.

So, we told our attorney and DCYF that we were on hold until further notice.

Now, it was just a waiting game.

We heard nothing from the local birth family, the church connection. So, we continued to pray for the birth parents and the difficult discussions they must be having.

I had almost daily texting conversations with Lexi. Her pregnancy was tumultuous. She was having a lot of bleeding. When she went in to see the doctor, they could see that both babies were growing, but Baby A's heart rate was down much lower than Baby B's heart rate. The birth mom also had the stomach flu, the regular flu, and many days of intense morning sickness and vomiting during a short span of time.

In addition to all of that, she was getting intense pressure from all her relatives to abort. Some absolutely horrible things were being done and said to her. She was threatened to be thrown out on the street if she did not abort her babies and was told, "The babies go or you go." She was only eighteen! So sad.

At one point, she gave in to the pressure from her family and made an appointment at Planned Parenthood. I didn't know about this. However, I was sitting on my bed on a Saturday afternoon and felt a nudge to send some flowers, chocolate, and balloons to her workplace on her birthday as a gift. She was turning nineteen on Monday, so I set them up to be delivered that morning.

On Monday evening, two phone calls came in. One was from my friend Kelly. She told me how the birth mom received our birthday gift and it so completely touched her that she canceled the appointment at Planned Parenthood that was scheduled for that Friday. We didn't even know there was an appointment, but there was and it was now canceled!! HALLELUJAH!

The second call came from the birth mom's foster mom—the one she had when she was fifteen. This woman was a Godly woman and she reached out to me to share a story. She proceeded to tell me that this birth mom received our gift and was blown away by it. No one in her family wished her a happy birthday or called her or even texted her. No one from her family purchased anything for her or celebrated her in any way that day. However, when she received our gift, she realized that there ARE really good people out there and realized we would be great parents for her babies.

Let the CONSEQUENCES of your OBEDIENCE be left up to GOD.

Oswald Chambers

The next morning, I talked to the birth mom on the phone. Showing emotion is a bit hard for her, but through her sadness and brokenness, I could hear her thankfulness. I could hear that she felt loved. I made it very clear to her that while we cared for her, it was GOD who loved her so much that He wanted her to be celebrated on her birthday. God told me to send her those gifts. I was just obedient. I told her how much God loves and cares for her!

I spent the next couple of days crying randomly as I processed how God had just used my obedience as a way to save two babies' lives! That was powerful!

Over the course of the next few weeks, we just walked alongside Lexi, whom God so deliberately placed in our lives. I was there to help put out fires in her life created by family members on a daily basis. One day she wanted to abort the babies, the next she wanted to raise the babies, and the next day she was putting them up for adoption. All along, she really knew what she wanted with those babies, she was just so torn and conflicted because of the hurt and verbal brutality of her family.

> *Ordinary people who faithfully, diligently, and consistently do things that are right before God will bring forth extraordinary results.*
>
> Elder David A. Bednar

January 12, 2015:

We received an email this week from the couple from church who connected us to the local birth parents. The couple from church wanted to know if we were willing to meet with the birth dad. We said we were and scheduled a meeting.

January 17, 2015:

We met with the couple from church, as well as the birth dad and his brother, who was there as support and as an interrogator. We spent the next four hours being "interviewed" and shared our photo albums with them. We answered their questions as openly and honestly as we could. The meeting went well, but we were firmly told that the birth parents have not yet made a decision. They said, "Please don't get your hopes up. They just want to meet you." Just prior to leaving the meeting, we threw the ball back into their court and said, "You know how to find us. We will not reach out to anyone. If you want to move forward, just contact us. We don't want you to feel any pressure from us." With that, we all hugged and left.

Conversation and life with the birth mom in Massachusetts continued on as usual. I provided a lot of emotional support and was falling in love with this young girl. I spent a lot of time helping her process all the hurtful things her family was putting her through, helping her find her a place to live, etc. Then I got a text from her ex-boyfriend, who thought she might be considering abortion again. Not long after that, I got a text from her that confirmed what he thought. She had made another appointment with Planned Parenthood. That upcoming week was a long week emotionally. They only perform abortions on Fridays in that particular area, or at least at the clinic where she was going. So, her abortion was scheduled for the following Friday. I put out prayer requests as far and wide as I could. I had people in Australia, South Africa, Canada, and all over the US praying for her and for her babies!

We all spent so much time praying for her. The intensity of our prayer and our encouragement was palpable. And we kept loving on her that week— finding a place for her to live and ways to get her some help.

February 5, 2015:
On Thursday night, she allowed me to call her and pray with her. I even found a few pro-life videos to show her what her sweet babies looked like. She was just shy of ten weeks. These videos were of real live babies in the womb. Jason was amazing and allowed me to spend the whole night in my room quietly helping her and encouraging her, praying with her. He took care of the kids downstairs for the night. As the phone call was coming to an end, I told her I was going to be snowboarding with the kids the next day and would not be available to talk because of poor cell phone reception on the

mountain. I told her I would contact her when I was home to find out the decision she made. I felt heavy, but I had to just leave it in God's hands.

February 6, 2015:

I woke up that Friday morning and started getting my kids ready for snowboarding on the mountain. Around nine, right as I needed to leave my house, I got a text from Kelly, who was spending just as much time and effort in this fight. She asked if I saw Facebook. I said no, and she proceeded to tell me that the birth mom had posted "It is off" and tagged several of us!

It was off. The three most beautiful words I had ever read!

As I drove the kids to the mountain that morning, I listened to the song "You Make Me Brave" by Bethel Worship. I had given the birth mom that song to listen to earlier in the week. And as I listened to it that morning while driving with the kids, I began to cry. Tears streamed down my cheeks as I realized the gravity of what was taking place! Those babies would remain ALIVE that day! Hallelujah! I felt she was brave and I felt God made me brave to fight so tirelessly all week. The kids were looking at me trying to figure out why I was crying so hard and I just couldn't hold it in. I had to tell them why this day was so important. The significance of the decision that young mom had made. The ramifications for the lives of those babies . . . it was so overwhelming!

Here's the thing—it wasn't even for us. We still were not told we were getting these babies. This was simply an all-out pro-life moment for those babies and that birth mom.

February 8, 2015:
That Sunday, the birth mom hit ten weeks and both babies were still alive and kicking around in that cozy little womb and growing like weeds. Hallelujah!

February 10, 2015:
On Tuesday, I was at our homeschool co-op when I received an urgent text from the church couple who put us in contact with the local birth parents. The wife wanted to know if she could meet with Jason and me immediately. I told her Jason was working at our house and I was nearly an hour away from him in Nashua at the co-op. I told her that I was free to talk if she wanted to meet me at my location. She instantly replied, "Okay, I'm hopping in the car now and will be to you in thirty minutes."

I snuck into the bathroom and prayed, "Lord, I don't know why she's coming all the way down here in such a hurry but help me to accept whatever she has to tell me."

About one minute before she arrived my phone rang. It was our adoption attorney, Margaret. Yes, the attorney who wasn't supposed to call with any more situations. She had another situation for us. There was a young teen mom who was due in February and only wanted a married Christian family. Our attorney was going to automatically match us with her if we said yes. Within seconds of getting off the phone with her, the wife (from the church) entered the building.

We hugged and she blurted out, "I'm not going to beat around the bush. I'm just going to tell you."

Now, I had really convinced myself that she was coming all the way down to soften the news that the couple decided to keep the twins or go with someone else. Being pro-parenting, we would've been okay with that. I was mentally prepared for that answer. I prayed in the bathroom. I was ready for it.

But I was NOT ready for what she said next. She said, "You're getting them. They've decided to put the babies up for adoption and they want you guys to parent them!"

My jaw hit the floor; I felt like I was in another world. Did she really just say we were getting the babies? Twin boys?

Yes, she did!

I felt badly because after she left I realized I had not responded as she may have been expecting me to respond. She was probably expecting tears and elation, but I was just in shock. I was composed while she was there, but after she left I sat in silence, replayed it all in my mind, and just became giddy. And, yes, I cried.

February 13, 2015:

Fast-forward a few days. The young mom in Massachusetts texted me and asked me if we could meet somewhere to talk in person. I said yes. So, on Friday we met at a restaurant half-way between us and discussed adoption details. I asked her some tough questions about her plans to abort and her plans to parent. She said she doesn't want to consider abortion an option any longer! Thank You, Jesus! We had a lovely and honest conversation. We laughed and enjoyed each other's company.

Later that evening she texted me and told me, "I have something to say to you."

I replied, "Uh-oh, that doesn't sound good. Is everything okay?"

She responded, "I want you guys to adopt the babies."

Come on. Is this how we were going to end four years of heartache and several failed adoptions? Could this be God's best?

Consider our socks knocked OFF!

Just for good measure, our attorney called on that same day and gave us yet another situation. A baby that was already born and in need of a home. He was still in the NICU in Arizona and had club feet. We had to say no. We were definitely at our limit with babies to adopt!

****

Blog Post
4/27/15
Baby A Miscarries

Over the last couple of weeks, the birth mom in Massachusetts has had a rough time. Her ex-boyfriend informed her he will NOT sign papers that will allow her to put the babies up for adoption. That same weekend, she got food poisoning or the stomach bug and was very ill.

All of that possibly led to a miscarriage of one of the babies. Baby A was already not doing too well, but between stress and several bouts of the stomach flu, the birth mom lost the baby. Baby B's heart rate was down a bit but still looks healthy. We continue to pray for her. She is thirteen weeks pregnant with Baby B. She is very sad and not doing well with this news.

February 28, 2015:
Adoption attorneys are now involved with the local New Hampshire couple (the church connection), and legal documents are being drawn up. The birth mom is at thirty-three weeks tomorrow, March 1. I will be thirty-eight years old on March 2. I can't believe we will be starting parenthood all over again at thirty-eight! We will have a fourteen-year-old and newborns! I know people have done crazier things, but we also know God has called us to do this. So, we faithfully follow the path God puts in front of us.

We have discussed baby names for the boys and I think we finally have our names:

Joel Christian, which means "He that wills or commands; Christ-bearer or Christ follower."

Micah Justin, which means "Messenger from God; just, upright, righteous."

So now it's just a waiting game. At thirty-three weeks, it really could be any day now. The birth mom went into labor three weeks ago, but the doctors were able to stop the labor, and she's been on bed rest since then. There is so much we need to do, but we aren't doing anything because we are just so afraid of not getting the babies and having done all that work for nothing. So, we will get them and have absolutely nothing, at all, prepared. Nothing. I cannot tell you how much that stresses me out. I'm a "ducks-all-in-a-row" kind of girl and there were no ducks lined up in preparation for bringing home two babies.

But, it is what it is. We will just rejoice in the adoption and pray for some help to come along in those first few days to help us get things up and running again. The biggest issue will be getting a new car that fits in our garage.

****

Blog Post
4/27/15
Baby B Miscarries

Difficult days . . .

March 20, 2015:
Baby B miscarried yesterday.

The poor birth mom is devastated. That sweet girl has known more loss in her short nineteen years than most people will know in a lifetime. She lost her sweet baby Ethan in December, then Baby A in February, and Baby B in March at nearly sixteen weeks.

Please keep this sweet young lady in your prayers. My heart is so heavy for her. Though she could not parent these babies, she loved them. She wanted the best for them. She wanted life for them. She is really hurting.

I have shared the Good News of Jesus with her and told her I would pray with her whenever she was ready. I want to see her start with a personal relationship with Jesus. We gave her a Bible with her name printed on the front. Now, we just continue to pray for her. I grew to love this young lady so much. My heart aches for her and all I want to see is joy and happiness in her life.

****

Blog Post
4/27/15
{The Twins Are Almost Due}

March 30, 2015:

It's almost time for the boys to be born. As a family, we are reserved after so many heartaches and failures, but there is a sense of excitement and hope in the air. A few baby outfits have been purchased, but other than that, nothing else. We will wait this out this time.

We sleep every night with our phones turned on, waiting for that "middle of the night" phone call. I battle with some anxiety that something bad will happen to them, but the couple from church prays with me and I sense peace settling in my mind.

April 6 is the scheduled C-section when she will be thirty-eight weeks. Now it's just a waiting game. Will they come prior to that or will they make it to that date?

We will continue to pray for them, their birth parents, birth grandparents, and the delivery.

We will wait upon the Lord in this time.

****

Blog Post

5/18/15

We're Now a Family of 8!

With God, ALL things are possible!!!

Well, we've finally made it. We've made it to six kids and we are still, most days, in disbelief about how it came about.

Here's the rest of the story . . .

It was actually the grandmother who approached Jason at church back in December about this possibility to adopt. Her son and daughter-in-law discovered they were expecting twins and, for reasons of their own, decided they could not raise these babies.

We met with them in January for the four-hour interrogation (remember?), and then it was the grandmother who drove down to Nashua while I was at our homeschool co-op to tell me they had picked our family to adopt their babies.

From that point on, it was all about the legal process. Their adoption attorney, our adoption attorney, papers, etc. The birth mom went into early labor but the doctors were able to stop it. And, like a champ, she managed to make it all the way to thirty-eight weeks carrying twin boys. By the time they were born, they needed no assistance. They were perfect!

April 6, 2015: Delivery Day

The alarm went off at 6:00 a.m. on Monday, April 6. We all started to wake up, shower, pack, and get ready to leave the house by seven in order to arrive at the hospital by 7:45. We made our way up to The Birth Place and met up with the boys' Nana, Pépé, and Uncle R. The attorney for the birth family (who happened to be the aunt of the birth father) was with the birth mom and dad as they prepped for the C-section.

We brought all four kids that morning, including their school work (yes, I was THAT mean homeschooling mama who made her kids do school, even on the day their baby brothers were being born!), their various activities to keep them busy all day, my overnight bags, etc. Since our crew also included Nana, Pépé, and Uncle R, we decided it was best to wait it out in the cafeteria. So, we loaded up our arms and headed downstairs.

Once we got down there, Nana, Pépé, Uncle R, and I all sat around a table in the middle of the hospital cafeteria and held hands and started to pray. Jason eventually joined us and we continued to pray for the delivery, the safety of the birth mom and those babies, as well as the difficult day ahead of them. This was a really meaningful moment.

We had finished praying and were chatting when we heard the lullaby song play over the hospital speakers. Every time a baby is born at the hospital, they play a lullaby song throughout the entire hospital so everyone can hear that a baby has just been born. We all smiled and wondered if that was one of our babies. Within moments, another lullaby played. Jason looked at his watch and said, "It's 8:16 a.m., I think the boys were just born."

Nana looked at me with tears in her eyes and said, "I think your babies are here, Bethanee!" We hugged. She was so sweet and so wonderful. I cannot tell you how very blessed we are that the boys will have their praying Christian grandparents in their lives!

Now at this point, I'm still not showing a lot of emotions. My heart is just too afraid of getting crushed again. We had made it this far and to lose them now would be yet another major blow for our family, especially because Jason and I had already said that if this one failed, we were done. Completely done trying to adopt. This was it—the last attempt.

We had no confirmation that those two lullabies were our boys, so we just continued to wait and talk. Uncle R finally said he was going to go upstairs to try to find his brother and get an update. Within minutes, Nana received a text from Uncle R that confirmed those lullabies were, in fact, our boys. The birth mom and babies were all doing well!

While waiting to go up to meet the boys, we received an email from Uncle R. It was a letter he had written to Jason and me and to the boys in the days leading up to this day. The letter was beautiful and so beautifully articulated. So much emotion and heart went into that letter. We are so thankful to have that from him. We will show it to the boys when they grow up and are old enough to understand.

Roughly fifteen to twenty minutes after receiving the text telling us they were born, the birth dad's aunt, also the attorney for their family, came downstairs and pulled the four of us adults to the side with a very serious tone. She explained that while the babies were being checked out in the NICU—a mandatory rule since they were twins—the head nurse for the NICU and the hospital social worker went into the birth mom's recovery room alone. While it was just the three of them, these women began trying to convince the birth mom to change her mind. While we do not know what was said, we do know this caused a lot of problems. Once the birth father realized all of this was happening, he quickly went in to support the birth mom. She was very upset by this, which also made birth dad and the aunt/attorney very upset too.

That started a flurry of legal conversations between the birth parents' attorney, our attorney, and the hospital social worker. It was tense for a while, but in the midst of it being very tense, we were assured that mom was confident in her decision. She knew this was the decision she wanted to make and was not changing her mind.

For the record, we would've been okay if she had changed her mind. Heartbroken, but okay. These were her precious boys, and we understood that feeling as parents.

Fifteen to twenty minutes later, after the commotion died down, the aunt/attorney came downstairs to get Jason and me. She asked if we would like to meet our sons. Our sons!!!

I'm crying again, just typing this.

Nana and Pépé, as we now lovingly call them, said they would stay behind in the cafeteria with our big kids. Jason and I were escorted to the NICU to see the boys. As we entered the NICU the aunt/attorney whispered, "That's her, the head nurse." Instantly, I felt anger rise up in me. I did not want to see her nor speak to her. I knew what she had tried to do and I wanted nothing to do with her. As she introduced herself and tried to shake my hand, I just started to cry. She banded my wrist with two bands, one for each baby. I wiped my tears away but could not bring myself to speak to her. I was so afraid I would say something I would regret. She led us down the long hallway to the room where the boys were.

Let me set the scene here. Their room was right next to the nurses' station, which had a huge glass window opening right into the twins' NICU room. There were about ten nurses all standing in the nurses' station watching this whole situation unfold.

We turned and walked through the doorway and there they were. Each tiny little boy under his own warmer, swaddled in hospital blankets with matching hats. Out of the corner of my eye, I could see ALL of the nurses staring at us through the

215

window, but I couldn't tell why. "Are they angry with us? Do they disapprove? Heck, I don't care!" This was our adoption! And I didn't need their approval!"

We stood over one of the boys for a moment, just staring. I started weeping and "ugly" crying as I stared at them. Jason just held me. I finally asked the nurse if I was allowed to hold them and she said yes. So, I gingerly scooped up a baby. She walked over and got the other baby and handed him to Jason. I think I was holding Landon and Jason was holding Micah, but I can't be certain even to this day.

The only documentation we have of this moment comes from the amazing attorney on their side, the aunt. She asked if we wanted her to take a picture. I will forever treasure the picture of that precious moment!

Jason and I sat in that room, holding the boys, staring at them in disbelief, and discussing the events that had taken place over the last three months. We compared babies and tried to find differences between them. The doctors and nurses were all unsure if they were identical or fraternal twins. During the ultrasound, the birth mom was told they were fraternal twins because they did not share a placenta. After they were born, however, the doctor that came in to check on them said that was ridiculous. Twins can still be identical even if they don't share a placenta. So, Jason and I tried to find differences just so we can tell them apart. It was difficult. I thought their noses and head shapes were ever so slightly different, as did Jason.

But it was slight at best. They looked identical to us. [After they were home, just because we were curious, we did have them tested and they were a near 100 percent perfect match, 99.99999999999% DNA match. They are identical.]

Jason and I were moved to the room where we would be staying for the duration of the boys' hospital stay—right across from the nurses' station. Again, I felt like we were in a fishbowl being watched the whole time.

Once we were in our new room, the attorney/aunt went and got our four older kids. We heard them coming down the hallway and could hear the excitement in their voices. Finally, they turned the corner and walked into the room. Their reactions were so cute! Two of them went to one of the boys and the other two went to the other boy. So much joy and love filled that room. It was beautiful.

They each took turns holding the babies. Caleb was holding one of the babies and was just staring at him. I walked over to Caleb, bent down, and whispered in his ear, "What do you think, Caleb? You finally have brothers." He leaned down, kissed that baby, and just started to cry. My heart melted and I began to cry too (as I'm doing now). I was so happy for him. He had wanted a brother for so long.

As the day continued, Nana K, Pépé R, and Uncle R all joined us in welcoming the babies into our family. They all did the same things we did, trying to figure out differences between the two boys, and just smiled and watched them as they squeaked and stretched.

Uncle R said his final goodbye. That was such a tender moment. I guess in a show of solidarity and support for his brother he made a commitment to not be a part of their lives. If his brother couldn't be in their lives, he would honor his brother and also not be in their lives. So as Uncle R held Landon and said his final goodbye, he kissed him on the forehead, tears streaming down his face, then handed him over to me. The snapshot of this memory in my head makes me cry again now. It was so sweet. So tender. So sad. We are always more than happy to allow Uncle R to see them, but we greatly respect the decision he has made for his brother's sake. What a sacrifice of love. Uncle R was incredibly amazing throughout all of this. He loves his little brother and these babies so much.

After all of the goodbyes with the birth family, it was just our happy little family of eight for the rest of the day. We were all in a little bit of shock, a tad cautious, and very overwhelmed with our love for the boys and for the birth family. We were and still are keenly aware of the huge sacrificial love they had to make the adoption happen.

In the early evening Jason decided to take the kids home for some dinner. He still had to purchase formula, car seats, and a stroller (all things we waited on this time). He would be gone for the rest of the night so it was just the boys and me at the hospital. The commotion of the day had ended, almost.

Around 4:30 p.m. I was told that the birth mom wanted to meet the boys. She had hired a professional photographer to take pictures of them and wanted to say her goodbyes to them. Jason and I had mentally prepared for that time. We prayed that the birth mom would have the closure she needed, and that she would feel at peace with her decision. We were told the boys would go upstairs to see her around 6:00 p.m.

At 5:25 p.m., the aunt/attorney came into my room and said the birth mom wanted to meet me. That was a change in plans. Up until that point, I had only met the birth dad, Uncle R, and the grandparents. So, when the aunt came in and said the birth mom wanted to meet me I said, "Okay."

Then the aunt said, "Okay, let's go."

Whoa. I was taken aback. "She wants to meet me now? Like, right now?"

The aunt responded, "Yes. Are you okay with that?"

"Surrrre."

I was processing so many emotions and felt like a ball of nerves, as I suspect hers were too. My stomach was in knots and my mind was racing. *What do I say? Will she like me or hate me? What if I say something wrong? What if she cries? What will I say? Will I be able to hold it together? What if I cry?* and on and on and on.

I walked into her room where it was just her, the birth dad, Uncle R, and the aunt/attorney. I walked right over to her and hugged her. Words escaped me; all I remember is us crying together. We made some small talk (of which I can remember very little). We talked about Jason's and my journey of trying to have kids and adopt children, they asked if we had a car large enough to fit our whole family in, then she asked me what the boys' names were going to be. At that moment, I was able to share with her that we partially named the boys after her and her husband. The boys' middle names are slightly altered versions of their first names. We were so honored to do that. I don't even know how they felt about it, but I know it makes us happy that the boys have a piece of their birth parents in their name.

So, their finalized names are Landon Justice and Micah Christian.

Just as our time was coming to a close, the birth mom's mother arrived. She did not want to meet me and was having a very difficult time processing all of it. I get it. She was griev- ing her own loss. As soon as she walked through the door, I stood up and hugged her. I told her it was nice to meet her and then I said goodbye to everyone in the room. The birth mom and I hugged goodbye and I hugged her mom again. The aunt walked back to my room where the boys were waiting. As soon as I arrived back in the room, the aunt, a nurse, and the boys all went to the birth mom's room. I was told pictures would take about forty-five minutes to an hour and then the boys would be back. I texted Jason and told him the boys had gone up.

So, there I sat, in my room, all by myself. My mind was all over the place. Feeling SO eternally grateful to have met her, hugged her, talked with her, and cried with her. So grateful to feel like she and I both had some sense of closure and peace because of that meeting. Simultaneously, my mind was aware that she now was in the presence of both babies and she could change her mind—especially after having just met me (again, not knowing if she liked me or not).

I decided to go grab some dinner in the cafeteria. I ate quickly and returned by the time the boys should've been arriving back in my room. I walked in and the room was empty. No babies. My heart sank.

"Okay, Bethanee, pray."

My prayer was not for me or for us. It was for this sweet and loving birth family who was undoubtedly dealing with a lot of emotions. Turmoil in one of the greatest senses, in a way no other person on earth can understand. How do you let go? How do you say that final goodbye, knowing what you're losing? I just began to pray. I called Jason and asked him and the kids to be praying. With all transparency, we were also praying that our hearts would not get crushed.

Another full hour passed and the boys were still upstairs with the birth family. Not with me. My heart was sinking. Jason was texting often. Finally, at eight, I went out and asked one of the nurses if they had any information. She called upstairs to get an update. About three minutes later I was told the boys were on their way back down to me.

As soon as the boys arrived back in my room, the attorney/aunt apologized for how long it took. She said the professional photographer they hired to take pictures of the boys showed up an hour and fifteen minutes late. They were unsure if the photographer was going to come at all, so they started taking photos with their phones. Then the photographer finally arrived and took all the pictures she needed to take. As the time came to an end, they all hugged, kissed, and said goodbye to the boys. I was told the grandmother asked the birth mom, "Will you have the boys brought up tomorrow before they go home?" to which the birth mom responded something of this sort, "No, I've said my goodbyes. I have peace."

Respect. Awe. Sadness. Relief.

It was about 8:30 pm and I was changed into my PJs, ready to wind down the day in my room with the boys. I closed the privacy curtain so the nurses could no longer see me through the glass window. I gently took both babies out of their bassinets and sat on the bed with them. This was my moment with them. The moment I had been waiting for all day. My time to be alone with them, to introduce myself to them, to hug them, kiss them, and tell them how much I loved them and had been waiting and praying for them.

I stared at those two sweet, tiny babies and I began to cry (shocker, I know!). Yes, there was still a possibility the birth mom could change her mind, but Jason and I were both feeling pretty confident. Waves of tears slowly rolled down my cheeks as I just sat and stared at them, held them, and fed them. So much joy. So much closure. So much peace. So much love.

Not for a moment did I love them any less than if I had given birth to them myself. Not for a moment did I question whether these were my boys. They were my boys and I was their mom.

Several people have asked, "Why did the birth mom give them up?" or "How could she do that? I could never do that!"

Please understand this, birth parents do not just give their babies away. They do not just give them up. They painstakingly, lovingly, methodically, and with great care, concern, and more love than we can even begin to imagine PLACE them into an adoptive home. Our birth parents placed these babies into our home. They chose us. They made a HUGE sacrificial choice to love their boys, our boys, more than they loved themselves.

Here's one of my favorite quotes from a birth mom who so beautifully sums up adoption:

I placed my baby for adoption, and I can say he's the best thing that ever happened to me. He transformed my life. I loved my child more than words can explain, and I still do. I believe my love for him was the first real love I'd ever felt, because it was completely self-less. It was the BIGGEST feeling I've known. My heart grew in my chest the moment I laid eyes on him. Had I loved him any less—one ounce less—he would be with me now! My love for him was the only thing that could enable me to break my own heart. I didn't just feel love; I did what love dictated.

~ Tamra, birth mother

Having met our birth parents, I do not doubt, for one minute, this is exactly how they felt and continue to feel. They loved these little guys so deeply that they thought it would be best to place them in another home, in our home.

We are blessed.

We took the boys home the next day, April 7, 2015. We had to wait for a court-appointed date so the birth mom could terminate her parental rights and sign them over to us. That court date occurred on Monday, April 20, exactly two weeks after the boys were born. We woke up praying that morning. We were praying for the birth family as we knew they were finalizing the most difficult decision of their lives. We prayed for God to reveal His heart for them, and for these boys.

We were not allowed to be present during the signing, but we were told by our attorney that the court appearance was extremely emotional and difficult. We received the call around 11:30 a.m. It was official.

The boys were ours. They were Syversens!

It was a bittersweet journey. We were so very happy as a family to know they were ours and all of this, the last (nearly) four years of trials and tribulation, was finally ending. However, we were overcome with sadness for the birth family as we knew that being brave and loving so sacrificially meant they were in great pain that day. Love and bravery don't always look the way we think they do, but birth parents are brave and they love deeply.

If you made it this far and you are still up for a little reading, then I would encourage you to read the following powerful article posted on The Huffington Post: "Dear Mom of an Adopted Child." As an adoptive parent, I could relate to so much in this article. So, I'm hoping it's a source of encouragement to you too.

> *LOVE is the tie that BINDS this Family TOGETHER.*

CHAPTER 15

LOOKING BACK

I am who I am today because of all I endured. And I still carry the tender scars. But I have grown to understand God and His timing better than ever.

God was faithful—not because we got what we wanted or because we ended up with six kids, but because He was with us the entire time. We prayed and asked for doors to be closed, and they closed. We prayed and asked for answers to our prayers, and we got answers in some form or another.

At the end of the adoption for both boys—the adoption had to be handled as two separate adoptions because they are two separate people—we received the bill from Margaret, our attorney. This bill—the total cost of the adoption for both boys—was almost the *exact same dollar* amount raised among our friends that one day, combined with the amount Margaret had given back to us for the failed adoption. Eight thousand dollars was raised, and the cost for both boys' adoption was eight thousand dollars TOTAL. God made a way. God will *always* make a way, if it's in His plan and His will.

And this is how He made a way for us with such low adoption costs: we "found" the adoption situation ourselves and we brought it to Margaret. The birth dad's aunt was an attorney and offered to do all the work on her end, pro bono, as a courtesy to her nephew and his wife. It was a local adoption, so no traveling was needed. And even though some of our fundraisers resulted in just a couple hundred dollars, they added up to nearly the *exact* dollar amount we needed. One couple, close college friends of ours, Brian and Kristen Johnsen (who now have 4 adopted children as of January 2019) had been saving up for their own adoption but God was bringing children from DCYF into their family. They both felt a prompting from God to give their adoption funds to us, so with prayer and love, they wrote a check for two thousand dollars! *God made the way.* He knew exactly what was needed and He provided it for us. God is always faithful.

Trials will always come in life, but my question for you is this: *What will you do in the midst of those trials? And what will you allow God to do?* I really struggled after we lost Eliana. I needed to know and understand God in a way that I had not yet known Him before. I had to ask myself the hard questions like *Does God exist?* even though it scared me. Asking those questions allowed me to really understand my beliefs and the foundation of my faith. I read the Bible like never before and I rediscovered the foundation of my childhood faith.

Looking back, if I could encourage the younger version of myself—that woman who desperately wanted to start a family—I would say to myself, *"Bethanee, trust God and His plan. Don't go ahead of Him. Wait on Him and keep praying. It's okay to be angry and sad in the midst of a storm, but then look up to see what God is doing. Don't stay in that place of anger and sadness for too long* *because God is writing a magnificent story and creating an exquisite tapestry. **It will be His story and yours to tell.** "*

Our children and all their stories, including the pain and the tears, have a purpose. I believe, in the midst of those really hard times, God was "pulling up His sleeves" and saying, *"Okay my sweet daughter, I'm working on this. I'm writing this story and I'm going to trust your family to eventually tell My story."* Not necessarily in this book, but in our everyday relationships and random encounters; on the radio, at birthday parties and dinner parties, at philanthropic Events and so on. So, wherever we are, Jason and I tell people about God's story for our family because this is God's story and He's asked us to share it. Because of Him, we have six kids and a pretty amazing testimony of His grace and love.

> *And we know [with great confidence] that God [who is deeply concerned about us] causes all things to work together [as a plan] for good for those who love God, to those who are called according to His plan and purpose.*
>
> Romans 8:28 AMP

Infertility, recurrent miscarriages, and failed adoptions were all very hard emotionally, but I praise God for every single tear that fell and every single moment when I fell to the ground in pain, unable to breathe. Every single one of those moments made me who I am today and they redefined my relationship with God in the most pure and true way. These are the moments—in the valleys of life—when we really find out who we are. God drew me closer to Him and whispered, *"Daughter, I've got you. Give it to Me. Let Me carry your burdens. You will overcome this, by the blood I shed for you. You will see breakthrough and you will have a story unlike any other. Will you love Me no matter what? Will you pursue Me with all your heart, no matter what?"*

So now I'm asking you: Will you take your trials and your challenges and allow God to show you the purpose and plan He has for you and for His kingdom? Will you allow God to write your story—past, present, and future?

Author's Note

In the final months of the publishing of this book I was diagnosed with Celiac Disease (CD) (October 2018). Since this diagnosis, I have discovered that doctors are doing a lot of research and are finding ties to unexplained infertility and unexplained recurrent miscarriages to CD. CD is a serious automimmne disorder that affects the absorbotion of nutrients in the body. When an individual with CD consumes any gluten the body mounts an attack against the small intestines, which is where all the vital nutrients we eat are absorbed. Left untreated, CD can have lifelong consequences, one of those being infertility and recurrent miscarriages. It's too late to determine if gluten and CD were the cause of my infertility and miscarriages, but I felt I needed to add this in here in case you are a reader currently going through either or both of those situations. I did a short amount of research online about this and there are stories of women who removed gluten from their diet and shortly thereafter conceived and carried to term. I am not a doctor, nor am I giving any medical advice, but I was so saddened to know my 10 years of trying to conceive could've been alleviated by simply finding out about my CD and/or at least just cutting out gluten as a trial and error type of test. I hope this helps someone out. Let me know if it did. I'd love to hear about it. I also have a link on my website with some information regarding CD and infertility/recurrent miscarriages you can browse through. My prayers and heart are with each of you readers going through these struggles.

REFERENCE PAGE

1. www.resolve.org
2. www.verywell.com
3. NIV
4. NIV, emphasis added
5. NIV
6. NIV
7. www.adoptionsharethelove.com
8. www.GodVine.com
9. www.GodVine.com

CPSIA information can be obtained
at www.ICGtesting.com
Printed in the USA
LVHW112005030519
616636LV00001B/2/P